Praise for
Millennials Who Manage

"The one thing all Millennial managers lack is experience. They must combat that by being extremely sharp in every other arena. *Millennials Who Manage* provides critical insight and perspective that allows leaders to get into the mindset of those they are leading. There is a plethora of great books on management and leadership; however, most of them do not speak directly to Millennials. This book provided me with much needed insight, and it is a tool that I will continue coming back to over and over again."

—**Rob Knutsen**, CEO, J. Derek Lewis & Associates

"After working with Chip for half a decade on the topic of Millennials in the workforce, he never fails to deliver new insights, useful coaching, and overall value to everyone who is participating in the multigenerational workforce. He has been able to tailor the message to each segment in a respectful way right when they need it, and *Millennials Who Manage* is a great addition—again—right when they need it. Most workers don't wake up in the morning looking for ways to derail their career, but in fact they do just that. The multigenerational workforce is wrought with challenges, and Chip's expertise on the topic is unmatched in navigating the workplace of the present and the future."

—**Ron Weber**, Director of Service Delivery, ShiftGig

"You often hear managers bemoan their inability to understand or effectively manage their millennial staff, and many books have been written about how to understand Millennials. What has been missing in this space is a book that speaks to the Millennials themselves. As Millennials, we have the power to change the negative perceptions of our generation and to collaborate with coworkers across generations, and this book coaches Millennials to do just that. Career paths are becoming increasingly difficult to navigate and *Millennials Who Manage* is a practical guide for realizing your potential and avoiding pitfalls in the workplace while staying true to yourself. The book challenges Millennials not only to strive to be understood, but to consider that the perceptions of other generations are valid. This is especially important for those Millennials who find themselves challenged by the task of managing multi-generational teams. *Millennials Who Manage* encourages each of us to examine how our own values and assumptions are affecting our work and our communication style, with an emphasis on finding ways that we can work together. I'd love to see this book on the shelf of every young aspiring manager. I will certainly be utilizing the tools and tactics presented to sharpen and hone my own leadership skills."

—**Kendra Puryear**, Director of Development, Orange County United Way

"There is no escaping the fact that an ever increasing part of the work force is and will continue to be made up of Millennials both as employees and managers. Understanding what makes them tick and motivated is a must. Chip Espinoza's work in this field is ahead of the curve, groundbreaking, and should be required reading for anyone who desires to effectively manage in today's workplace…which is of course everyone!"

—**Jim McInnis**, Founder & CEO, RDR Sales Consulting

"How do we manage in the multi-generational workplace? Over the past 10 or so years, we have begun to enjoy the new expectations (and challenges) as Generation Y has entered the workforce with a bang! Now, as the early Millennials are hitting their 30s and beginning to take more senior management and leadership roles, things are shifting again.

"In this book, Chip Espinoza and Joel Schwarzbart give a thoughtful account on how to prepare oneself to lead and be lead in the four generation office. Packed full of practical advice, this book is a 'how to' guide to survive and thrive in our new world.

"If you are 3 years into your work life and about to lead a team of people who grew up loving rock and roll, then make sure this book is on your nightstand. Well written and avoiding the temptation to lapse into constant 'management speak,' it's a compelling read that you will find hard to put down.

"I look forward to my next boss being a Millennial!"

—**Paul Bowles**, Global Resourcing, Thales

"*Millennials Who Manage* is powerful on many levels. I manage people who are 10, 15, 20 years older than me. This book helped me understand why I have been experiencing so many disconnects with them and what I can do about it. The book is really helpful in explaining the perspectives of the different generations and why they cause so much friction in my department. It has practical suggestions for improving interactions across generations. As a director focused on getting stuff done, I really appreciate that."

—**Mei Shan Tan**, Director of Financial Planning & Analysis, Optum

Millennials Who Manage

Millennials Who Manage

How to Overcome Workplace Perceptions and Become a Great Leader

Chip Espinoza

Joel Schwarzbart

Publisher: Paul Boger
Editor-in-Chief: Amy Neidlinger
Acquisitions Editor: Charlotte Maiorana
Editorial Assistant: Olivia Basegio
Cover Designer: Chuti Prasertsith
Managing Editor: Kristy Hart
Project Editor: Elaine Wiley
Copy Editor: Kitty Wilson
Proofreader: Sarah Kearns
Indexer: MoJo's Indexing and Editorial Services
Senior Compositor: Gloria Schurick
Manufacturing Buyer: Dan Uhrig

© 2016 by Chip Espinoza and Joel Schwarzbart
Old Tappan, New Jersey 07675

For information about buying this title in bulk quantities, or for special sales opportunities (which may include electronic versions; custom cover designs; and content particular to your business, training goals, marketing focus, or branding interests), please contact our corporate sales department at corpsales@pearsoned.com or (800) 382-3419.

For government sales inquiries, please contact governmentsales@pearsoned.com.

For questions about sales outside the U.S., please contact international@pearsoned.com.

Company and product names mentioned herein are the trademarks or registered trademarks of their respective owners.

Printed in the United States of America

First Printing October 2015

ISBN-10: 0-13-408679-1
ISBN-13: 978-0-13-408679-8

Pearson Education LTD.
Pearson Education Australia PTY, Limited.
Pearson Education Singapore, Pte. Ltd.
Pearson Education Asia, Ltd.
Pearson Education Canada, Ltd.
Pearson Educación de Mexico, S.A. de C.V.
Pearson Education—Japan
Pearson Education Malaysia, Pte. Ltd.

Library of Congress Control Number: 2015910954

Contents

Chapter 1 **A Priori** 1

Why Read *Millennials Who Manage?* 3

Learning as a Way of Being 4

Managerial Leadership 5

Task- and Relationship-Oriented Leadership 6

Stereotypes and Generalizations 6

      Overcoming Stereotype Threat 7

Endnotes 9

Chapter 2 **Making the Transition into Management** 11

Welcome to Management 12

What Do You See as Positive About Being Managed by
    Someone Under 35? 13

What Do You See as the Downside About Being Managed by
    Someone Under 35? 14

What Management Advice Would You Give to a Manager
    Who Is Under 35? 16

Endnotes 17

Chapter 3 **Developing a Perspective** 19

The Concept of Dignity as a Mind-Set 21

Got Perspective? 24

Endnotes 24

Chapter 4 **Be True to You** 27

The Desire to Please Your Boss 28

It Is Inevitable That You Will Have a Disagreement with
    Your Manager 30

It Is Inevitable That Your Relationships with Peers Will
    Change When You Move into Management 32

The People Who Care About Us the Most Are the Ones
    Who Most Likely Will Hold Us Back 33

Organizations by Nature Exert a Powerful Force Against
    Self-Differentiation 34

Endnotes 36

Chapter 5   Be True to Others **37**

    It's Okay to Identify with People Your Age 37

    It's Okay to Identify with People Older Than You 38

    What Does It Mean to Be Authentic? 38

    Exploring Your Autobiography 39

    Returning to Your Roots 41

    Avoiding Comfort Zones 41

    Seeking Honest Feedback 42

    The Challenges of Being Authentic When Transitioning
        into a New Role 43

    You Have to Be Believed to Be Heard 45

    Endnotes 45

**Chapter 6   Generational Differences:
              Fact or Fiction?** **47**

    The Maturational Perspective 47

    The Life Course Perspective 48

        Generational Subcultures 50

    Defining the Generations 52

        The Silent Generation 53

        Baby Boomers 54

        Generation Xers 56

        Millennials 57

        All Together Now 59

    Endnotes 60

Chapter 7   Dynamics of a Multigenerational Workforce 63

    Perceptual Biases 70

    Identifying Biases in the Conference Board Results 71

    Something Else Going on Besides Just Overconfidence 73

    Communicate, Communicate, Communicate! 75

    Endnotes 76

Chapter 8   The Reasons You Will Be a Great Leader 79

    Millennial Manager Survey 80

    Endnotes 88

Chapter 9 **Managing Millennials** **89**

Some Advice About Giving Advice 89

Work Is Culture Shock 90

Managers Who Get It and Managers Who Don't 91

Manager Perceptions of Millennials 93

Managerial Leader Competencies Needed for
Managing Millennials 95

Be Flexible 95

Create the Right Rewards 96

Put Their Imagination to Work 96

Build a Relationship 96

Be Positive When Correcting 96

Don't Take Things Personally 97

Show the Big Picture 97

Include the Details 97

Make It Matter to Them 98

The Biggest Challenges Millennials Report Facing in the
Workplace 98

Lack of Experience 99

Not Being Taken Seriously 100

Not Getting Respect 100

Being Perceived as "Entitled" 100

Lack of Patience 100

Getting Helpful Feedback 100

Understanding Expectations 100

Miscommunication with Older Workers 100

Rigid Processes 101

Proving Value 101

Understanding Corporate Culture 101

Challenges Created by Perception 101

Coaching Millennials to Overcome Career Roadblocks 104

Managing Millennial Teams 106

Endnotes 108

Chapter 10 Managing Boomers, Xers, and Silents. 111

Recommendations for Managing Workers Older
Than Yourself. 113

Know What They Don't Like 113

Understand What Motivates Them 114

Seek Their Input, Learn from Them,
and Encourage Mentoring. 114

Communicate 115

Be a Leader but Don't Overdo the "Boss" Thing 115

Generation X 115

Baby Boomers 117

Silent Generation. 119

Endnotes. 120

Chapter 11 Getting to the Next Level. 123

Back Where We Started 123

Managing Your Impatience. 125

Avoiding the "Too Much, Too Soon" Mistake 126

Being Self-Giving Rather Than Self-Protecting. 128

Embracing Resistance. 129

Contentment Breeds Discontent. 131

Recognizing Sabotage. 133

Leadership-Centric Rather Than Leader-Centric Thinking . . 135

Following Your Followers 136

Being an Empowering Leader 137

The Over/Under on Communication. 139

Most Problems Are Not Problems at All 141

Change Is Everyone's Job. 142

Don't Be Afraid of Conflict 143

Stage 1: Tension Development 144

Stage 2: Role Dilemma 144

Stage 3: Injustice Collecting 144

Stage 4: Confrontation. 145

Stage 5: Adjustments 145

The Nature and Presence of the Leader 145

Everybody Gets Stuck. 146

Endnotes. 147

Index 149

Acknowledgments

Thank you, Lisa, Chase, Chance, Chandler, and Charli. You inspire and motivate me. Your support is invaluable. Thank you, Mom. You nurtured my love for words and the craft of organizing them. Thank you, Joel. I enjoyed collaborating with you on this book. Thank you to my colleagues at Concordia University Irvine. Thank you to my past, present, and future students. You have and will continue to influence my voice. Thank you to Dove Canyon Golf Club. You are my oasis. Thank you to Norman Shawchuck. I miss you. Save me a seat up there.

—Chip Espinoza

First, I want to thank the anonymous participants in our surveys. We live in an age of constant bombardment by marketers and researchers, and it is all too tempting to shut out strangers' solicitations for our time. Without the contribution of their thoughts and time, this book could not exist. We gained unique insights from our participants, for which I am deeply grateful.

I also wish to thank my students. Their questions and challenges motivated me to develop better ways to communicate the topics of organizational behavior. Their interest rewarded me for that effort.

I wish to thank my co-author Chip Espinoza. Through the course of this project and others, I have seen him work through many challenging situations with uncommon grace. Chip is an outstanding classroom teacher and trainer, but as a leader who practices what he preaches, he also teaches by example.

Finally, I thank my family, my wife, Ti-lien, and our children, Joshua and Annie, for their patience while I worked on this book. They cheerfully supported me while I took time on weekends and evenings to write.

—Joel Schwarzbart

About the Authors

Chip Espinoza, Ph.D., is the coauthor of *Managing the Millennials: Discover the Core Competencies for Managing Today's Workforce* and *Millennials@Work: The 7 Skills Every Twenty-Something Needs to Overcome Roadblocks and Achieve Greatness at Work*. He is also the Academic Director of the Organizational Psychology program at Concordia University Irvine.

Chip keynotes internationally and across the country on how to create an environment in which Millennials can thrive. Chip is a leading expert on the subject of generational diversity in the workplace. He consults in the civic, corporate, and non-profit sectors.

Chip has authored several articles on the subject of leadership and is the go-to person for news agencies on the topic of integrating younger workers into organizations. He is a content expert for CNN on the subject of generational diversity in the workplace. He has also been featured on Fox News, CBS Radio, and in major publications. Chip was named a Top 15 Global Thought Leader on the Future of Work by the *Economic Times*.

Joel Schwarzbart, Ph.D., received his doctorate in Social Science from the University of California at Irvine, where he studied Social Network Analysis. He teaches Organizational Behavior at Cal State University, Fullerton and has been studying the impact of Millennials on the workplace since 2006. Dr. Schwarzbart co-developed the Generational Rapport Inventory to measure strengths in managing across generations.

1

A Priori

Before you entrust your career to our advice, it is important that we let you know the background for this book and our qualifications for writing it. A student once asked me, "What qualifies you to teach this class?" It is a great question and deserves a reasoned response—and you might want to know the answer since you have plopped down the money to buy our book, invest the time to read it, and contemplate our advice.

We have been studying Millennials since they entered the workforce. Chip's doctoral dissertation was titled *Millennial Integration: Challenges Millennials Face in the Workplace and What They Can Do About Them.* He published *Managing the Millennials: Discover the Core Competencies for Managing Today's Workforce* in 2010 and followed it with *Millennials@Work: The 7 Skills Every Twenty-Something (and Their Manager) Needs to Overcome Roadblocks and Achieve Greatness* in 2014. *Millennials Who Manage* combines years of research and experience that will give you insight into how older workers perceive younger workers, competencies that are critical to managing your peers, challenges you face when managing people older than you, and potential roadblocks you may face when trying to advance to the next level.

From the outset, it is important for you to understand that our work is not a conversation *about* Millennials but rather a conversation *with* Millennials. Our mission has been to help create work environments in which Millennials can thrive. We love Millennials! The love affair started while teaching a course called Management Theory and Practice at the undergraduate level. We noticed a difference between our students in the 1990s and our students in the early 2000s. We noticed several differences, but one that especially stood out was that Millennials entered the classroom with the idea that everything is negotiable; they expected to have a voice with respect to assignments, absences, and even grades. While other faculty members experienced their students' desire to have a voice as off-putting, we recognized that Millennials wanted to succeed and desired to actively participate in the educational process. They wanted—sometimes even demanded—to be engaged. What more could a professor ask for?

It is one thing to notice a shift in student values and behaviors but quite another to commit personal resources and time to studying the phenomenon. The catalyst for committing wholeheartedly to the topic was one of Chip's classes flipping an assignment on him. The course was an elective listed as Emerging Management Theory. The goal of the course was to get students to realize that the subject of management is *sexy*—meaning management is not a static subject. It is incredibly dynamic because of the constant change in people, organizations, and the work environment. Also, management is the study of many different disciplines, including, among others, psychology, sociology, and anthropology. The students were encouraged to identify and write about what they considered an emerging challenge in the workforce and what they would do about it. The example Chip used at the beginning of the semester was what he viewed as the challenge of managing a generationally diverse organization. At the end of the semester, the students inspired (some would say provoked) Chip to actually begin researching and writing on the topic. The unmitigated truth is that his students were the catalyst for the work that led to the creation of this book and the two listed previously, all involving managing a multigenerational workforce.

Our ambition is for the voice of this book to be conversational and an easy read. Admittedly, it is a challenge writing in both the academic and business worlds. Some see academia as being "out of touch," while others argue that acting without critical systematic inquiry is "irresponsible." There can be tremendous value in both, and we see them as interdependent: Good theory informs good practice, and good practice informs good theory. We strive to be true to both worlds.

Why Read *Millennials Who Manage*?

We believe this book will resonate with you because it invites your engagement with the subject—you. People sometimes say that young managers are *blank slates* because they have less experience than older managers. But we don't visualize you as a *blank slate* on which we are writing. Nor are we concerned with convincing you to adopt our lens. You have a myriad of experiences and ideas that are already shaping your leadership perspective. Perhaps you have only recently hit the management ranks, but you have led in other contexts and also observed good and bad management. Those experiences are what Bruce Avolio refers to as the context of leadership learning—a person's life stream. He defines the *life stream* as the representation of events you accumulate from birth to the present that shapes how you choose to influence yourself and others. He reasons, "Keeping in mind the concept of one's life stream helps to keep leadership development in a state of becoming, until all of our streams, so to speak, run dry."[1] Hopefully, your leadership learning and development will be a lifelong process.

The intent of this book is to contribute to your life stream and ultimately to your effectiveness as a managerial leader. There will be some "how to," but there will be a lot more "how to be." Our hope is that while you are reading, you can immediately think of how to integrate your own thinking and person into what we are saying. It is through this process that your self-concept as a leader will become more defined and ultimately shape the framework for developing, organizing, and implementing your leadership skills.

A lot of early leader development literature placed the leader's primary focus on the follower. The objective was to teach the leader how to get the follower to do what she wanted him to do. The challenges of leading in today's world have caused, if not demanded, a shift in how we approach leader development. The primary focus of the leader is now on the self because it is the nature and presence of the leader that most impacts an organization.[2] Technical skills serve as the price of admission to leadership, but leading effectively depends on how well you negotiate the emotional and relational processes of what many refer to as both science and art.

Frances Hesselbein, co-editor of *The Leader of the Future*, says, "The three major challenges CEOs will face [in the 21st century] will have little to do with managing the enterprise's tangible assets and everything to do with monitoring the quality of: leadership, the work force, and relationships."[3] Hesselbein goes on to say, "The leader beyond the millennium will not be the leader who has learned the lessons of *how to do it....*The leader for today and the future will be focused on *how to be*—how to develop quality, character, mind-set, values, principles, and courage."[4]

We are not interested in inspiring you to change the face of management. That is going to happen with or without our help. We are more concerned with helping you develop a perspective that allows for personal change, adaptation, continual learning, and the ability to lead organizations worthy of human habitation. We want to assist you in your efforts to deploy your best self.

Learning as a Way of Being

One of the advantages younger workers feel they have in the workplace is being teachable. If you master nothing else, master learning. Liz Wiseman says that getting on the *learning curve* is more important than having experience in today's world of information overload and faster-paced work.[5] Aim to be on the learning curve not just through your professional formative years but your whole life; don't let your life stream go dry. Peter Vaill defines *learning* as the changes a person makes in himself or herself with respect to the *know-how, know-what,* and *know-why*.[6] We humbly add *know-how-to-be* to the list.

Organizations are not becoming less complicated. Every day they bring new learning challenges. Vaill explains, "Today's complex, interdependent, and unstable systems require continual imaginative and creative initiatives and responses by those living and working in them."[7] He is known for comparing management to maneuvering whitewater rapids. Here is what he has to say to anyone who wants to get into the management raft:

1. Permanent whitewater conditions are full of surprises.
2. Complex systems tend to produce novel problems.
3. Permanent whitewater conditions feature events that are "messy" and "ill structured."
4. Whitewater events are often costly.
5. Permanent whitewater conditions raise the problem of recurrence.[8]

Managerial Leadership

You will notice that the full title of this book has both the terms *manage* and *leader* in it. There are clear differences between the roles of management and leadership. Perhaps Bennis and Nanus offer the simplest distinction between the two: "Managers are people who do things right and leaders are people who do the right thing."[9] Some argue that you manage things and you lead people. Others would go so far as to say that management and leadership are such different functions that one person cannot do them both. The reality of organizational life is that at times, leaders manage and managers lead. Vaill touched on this by suggesting that the idea of a single person being called "the leader" or "the manager" is a myth.[10]

Although there are clear differences between leadership and management, our view is that you will find yourself in both roles. There is a lot of overlap between management and leadership. Vaill handles the convergence of roles with the title *managerial leader*. In a world that requires more with less, it is difficult to think that an organization can afford to separate the two roles. Therefore, we will not be making a distinction or emphasizing the differences between them. In the end, both roles involve getting people to attain certain objectives and goals. Not all managers desire to be great leaders. But isn't that a sad thought? Be different!

Task- and Relationship-Oriented Leadership

One area of overlap between management and leadership is giving attention to both tasks and relationships. Managerial leaders are often faced with the tension between getting things done and caring for the people with whom they work. The two orientations are not mutually exclusive but are often treated as such. Leaders who show little or no concern for their employees are often autocratic and risk demotivating or demoralizing their teams. Leaders overly concerned with everybody getting along may find it difficult to get things done or to hold people accountable for results. Great leaders emphasize both relationships and results. As a Millennial manager, you can expect to face the added complexity of generational dynamics when it comes to relating to and challenging your employees.

Stereotypes and Generalizations

This book contains a lot of generalizations. We realize that not all Millennials, Gen Xers, and Baby Boomers hold the same views or behave exactly as the stereotypes suggest. We also realize that not everyone born in 1979 is an Xer, nor is everyone born in 1980 all Millennial. Nevertheless, we will use the labels throughout the book. First, there are measurable differences anyone in a managerial role will benefit from understanding. Second, people treat one another according to those stereotypes rather than as individuals. For both reasons, it is therefore necessary to discuss them.

If you read just a few books or articles about Millennials or Xers, you will find a variety of dates used to demarcate the generations. Demographers tend to use the ranges 1946–1964, 1965–1977, and 1978–1999 as the birth years for the Baby Boom, X, and Millennial generations. These ranges correspond to peak, trough, and peak in the histogram of the number of babies born each year in the United States.

We prefer the date ranges 1943–1960, 1961–1979, and 1980–2000 as the birth years for Boom, X, and Millennial. We view generational "personality" as the product of macro social events. The events most impactful in shaping those personalities don't coincide exactly with the demographically determined dates. (We cover this in more detail in Chapter 6, "Generational Differences: Fact or Fiction?") Not all individuals are impacted by events in the same way or to the same degree. However, generational (or age cohort) experiences influence one's view of the world.

Overcoming Stereotype Threat

Historically, the focus of ageism was reserved for those in the twilight of their work life. But let's pause and look at the effect ageism may be having on the other side of the age spectrum.[11] Today's scholars are expanding the definition of ageism to "widely held beliefs regarding the characteristics of people in various age categories."[12] With that in mind, there may be a kind of reverse ageism in which younger workers are impacted by negative stereotypes.

Millennials are an easy group to identify in terms of their appearance and are therefore highly subject to being stereotyped. When a negative stereotype about a group is relevant to performance on a specific task, it is referred to as "stereotype threat."[13] An example would be "She is too young to handle the Walmart account." Individuals who are highly identified with a particular group may experience increased susceptibility to stereotype threat.[14]

Informal expectations can lead to stereotype threat against an individual and a group of individuals. A generation's attitudes, beliefs, and values play a role in the overall social construct. When we look at the formal age structure (i.e., where those who are older are in charge), power resides with older cohorts who share ideals about work attitudes, values, and behaviors. It can be argued that the larger the cohort (or group), the greater the influence over norms and expectations.

We don't want to let the cat out of the bag too early, but when we asked older workers in our survey, "What is the downside of being managed by a Millennial?," the second-most-frequent response was "dealing with their immaturity." In this case, the definition of *maturity* may be a generational construct. For instance, a 60-year-old manager could ride a bike through the office and have people see him as playful and fun—and even cheer him on. A Millennial could do the same thing but be considered immature and inappropriate. It can be incredibly frustrating, but you have to understand what is going on and learn to be proactive and not reactive.

Immaturity can mean a multitude of things. For the sake of our conversation, we would like to define it as a lack of self-regulation. Therefore, immaturity is the inability to act in your own long-term best interest or consistent with your deepest values. Self-awareness is critical to self-regulation in that it is the process of identifying, among other things, our values.

Overcoming negative perceptions has more to do with you learning about you than with others changing their opinions of you.

In the next chapter, we will discuss the difficulties of transitioning into management and share more results from our survey.

Endnotes

1. Avolio, B. J. (2005). *Leadership development in balance: Made/born*. Mahwah, NJ: L. Erlbaum, p. 13.

2. Friedman, E. H. (1985). *Generation to generation: Family process in church and synagogue*. New York: Guilford Press.

3. Hesselbein, F., Goldsmith, M., & Beckhard, R. (1996). *The leader of the future: New visions, strategies, and practices for the next era*. San Francisco: Jossey-Bass Publishers, p. 122–123.

4. Hesselbein, F., Goldsmith, M., & Beckhard, R. (1996). *The leader of the future: New visions, strategies, and practices for the next era*. San Francisco: Jossey-Bass Publishers, p. 123.

5. Wiseman, L. (2014). *Rookie smarts: Why learning beats knowing in the new game of work*. New York: HarperCollins.

6. Vaill, P. B. (1996). *Learning as a way of being: Strategies for survival in a world of permanent white water*. San Francisco: Jossey-Bass.

7. Vaill, P. B. (1996). *Learning as a way of being: Strategies for survival in a world of permanent white water*. San Francisco: Jossey-Bass, p. 5.

8. Vaill, P. B. (1996). *Learning as a way of being: Strategies for survival in a world of permanent white water*. San Francisco: Jossey-Bass.

9. Bennis, W. G., & Nanus, B. (1985). *Leaders: The strategies for taking charge*. New York. Harper & Row, p. 21.

10. Vaill, P. B. (1989). *Managing as a performing art: New ideas for a world of chaotic change*. San Francisco: Jossey-Bass.

11. Kalin, R., & Hodgins, D. C. (1984). Sex bias in judgments of occupational suitability. *Canadian Journal of Behavioral Science, 16*, 311–325.

12. Kalin R., & Hodgins, D.C. (1984). Sex bias in judgments of occupational suitability. *Canadian Journal of Behavioral Science, 16*, 311–325. p. 5.

13. O'Brien, L. T., & Hummert, M. L. (2006). Memory performance of late middle-aged adults: Contrasting self-stereotyping and stereotype threat accounts of assimilation to age stereotypes. *Social Cognition, 24*(3), 338.

14. Schmader, T. (2002). Gender identification moderates stereotype threat effects on women's math performance. *Journal of Experimental Social Psychology, 38*(2), 194–201.

2

Making the Transition into Management

While doing research for this book, we surveyed and interviewed Millennial managers in an attempt to identify difficulties they may have encountered while transitioning into management. We think their experience may be helpful to you on a couple of levels. First, the information will help you not feel alone if you have had similar experiences. Second, we can make you aware of what to anticipate about making the transition.

Not unlike transitioning from college to career, transitioning into management can be accompanied by a sense of loss—a loss of freedom and a loss of familiarity. There is something to be said for not having responsibility for others and for being able to blend into the fabric with friends. It is much more fun to critique than to be critiqued.

It is important to acknowledge the emotional components to making a transition. There are highs associated with achieving what you have been pursuing, but at the same time, you know you are leaving something behind. Christine Hassler refers to getting the blahs after achieving something you have always wanted to achieve as *Expectation Hangover*.[1]

Before sharing all the results of the survey, we'll share one bit of information: None of the respondents said that they wanted to forfeit their position and go back to the way things were pre-promotion.

Welcome to Management

In the survey, we asked, "What was the most difficult thing about transitioning into management?" In Table 2.1, we list the difficulties in order of frequency of response.

Table 2.1   Difficulties Millennials Experience When Transitioning into Management

The change in relational dynamics with peers
Being responsible for the work of others
Not being taken seriously
Getting people to listen
Delegating work
Holding people accountable
Motivating others

We want to draw attention to the items *not being taken seriously* and *getting people to listen.* You will see that the same labels show up in Table 9.4 in Chapter 9, "Managing Millennials." However, the reported challenges in Chapter 9 have to do with gaining the acceptance and respect of older workers. If you read the verbatim comments in the survey, *not being taken seriously* and *getting people to listen* are frustrations they have with older workers, peers, and younger workers. Feeling the pain? Millennials who manage have to struggle with getting respect from both ends of the age cohort spectrum.

In addition to asking Millennial managers about the challenges of transitioning into management, we also wanted to know how people experienced being managed by a Millennial. Again, our focus was to identify specific areas of development for our readers. We asked for the upside and the downside of being managed by a Millennial and what advice they would give a Millennial manager. The results along with verbatim comments are listed below.

What Do You See as Positive About Being Managed by Someone Under 35?

Table 2.2 shows the responses of respondents under and over 35 years of age to the question "What do you see as positive about being managed by someone under 35?" You will be able to see shortly some of the verbatim comments we received. In general, workers under 35 highly value Millennials' ability to relate, be helpful, be open-minded, and be understanding. Employees over 35 appreciated their energy, enthusiasm, open-mindedness, fresh perspective, and understanding of new technologies.

Table 2.2 Positives of Being Managed by Someone Under 35

They are relatable.
They have a fresh perspective.
They are open-minded.
They have energy and enthusiasm.
They understand new technologies.
They are helpful.
They are understanding.

Again, you will see similar labels show up in Chapter 9, this time in Table 9.6. It is obvious that Millennials trust these strengths and continue to build on them.

Here are a few verbatim remarks we got to this question:

> "Generally, the younger management tends to be less focused on micromanagement, and more focused on team building."

> "The person will probably have a different perspective and approach than an older manager and may know more about recent developments and newer techniques or technologies."

> "They are more open minded and willing to change."

"They are more 'with the times' and can relate to using technology that can make work easier and more efficient."

"They don't think you're stupid just because of your age or inexperience, at least they give you a shot to PROVE that you can do the job (or prove that you are stupid). They can explain things a little easier—training always goes smoother because they tend to understand what they are teaching instead of just reading out of a book."

"Currently, they are a breath of fresh air and much more trusting of all members in our group, who are adults with a lot of knowledge and experience. The previous manager of my current workgroup was approximately the same age, but was a micromanager."

"It feels less formal. I can speak in my own vernacular and it gets across (and vice versa). My manager being close in age also means that she can identify with what I'm experiencing in my own career development more than older managers would be."

"The positive about being managed by someone under 35 is their attitude and fresh perspective."

"Energy, enthusiasm, energy, enthusiasm, energy, enthusiasm... to the 10th power."

What Do You See as the Downside About Being Managed by Someone Under 35?

We know the answers to this question will not be news to you. As shown in Table 2.3, the number-one challenge Millennials face when entering the workforce is *lack of experience* (see Table 9.4 in Chapter 9). The *lack of experience* response may be a result of stereotyping and, if it were weighted, you would see that it is the opinion of most workers over 35 years old.

Table 2.3 Negatives of Being Managed by Someone Under 35

They lack experience.
They can be immature.
They have no long-term vision.
They are too focused on their next career step.
They struggle with people skills.

Here are a few (we'll spare you the repetition) verbatim remarks we received in response to this question:

> "They feel like they know everything but don't have the real experience."

> "My boss is smart but immature."

> "They have underdeveloped people skills."

> "She doesn't seem to be able to follow through on anything."

> "My boss is more concerned about his next position than the one he is in now."

The good news is that at this stage of your career, you *are* gaining valuable experience, learning from the experience of others, and understanding how to position yourself in the organization.

Experience is important, but it isn't always the greatest strength. Liz Wiseman, in her book *Rookie Smarts*, offers an interesting perspective on experience: "Sometimes the more you know, the less you learn. Too often experience can blind us to new possibilities and put us on the defensive. When we feel we already know what needs to be done, we are unwilling to coordinate our efforts with others or to accept outside input."[2]

What Management Advice Would You Give to a Manager Who Is Under 35?

The advice we got in response to this question (see Table 2.4) reflects what you would read on the flipchart at almost any training event for managerial leaders. You know the qualities you appreciate in the people who manage you. But what keeps us from being the leaders we want to follow? Where is the breakdown? It is not a question we want to answer for you. We want you to answer it for yourself. Your greatness is dependent upon it.

Table 2.4 Employee Advice for a Manager Under 35

Listen.
Be respectful.
Be patient.
Be a learner.
Treat employees as equals.
Lead by example.
Don't take on too much.
Be confident.

Here are some verbatim remarks we received in answer to this question:

> "Listen to those that are older than you; they may know about certain things that you don't and you can learn from each other."

> "Be kind. Be a real person. No bull#*&@. Just be yourself."

> "Learn the difference between being a boss and being a manager...a boss tends to micromanage, a manager leads by example and contributes to the workload."

> "Slow down. Work smarter, not harder; and treat your people the way you want to be treated to earn respect."

"Listen to what your employees have to say and take their opinions seriously."

"Be confident but respectful of all workers regardless of age."

The complexity of managing as a Millennial is captured by the last piece of advice—be confident. It is not an easy feat when you are perceived as inexperienced or immature. Confidence is the combination of self-efficacy and self-esteem. Self-efficacy is the belief that you are competent and that you have the tools to do the job. Self-esteem is the emotional evaluation of your own worth resulting in an attitude toward your self. Healthy self-esteem is evidenced by having the sense that you can cope with the challenges you will face and that you are worthy of the respect of others. Self-esteem without competency can lead to hubris (excessive pride or arrogance). The great news is that self-confidence can be built, and you are the one in charge. Sure, there is the outside influence of many different voices—some affirming and others not so much. In the next few chapters, we will help you better understand those voices. But more importantly, you will become more comfortable with your own.

In the next chapter, we will focus on the first step toward leadership greatness: developing your own leadership perspective.

Endnotes

1. Hassler, C. (2008). *20 something manifesto: Quarter-lifers speak out about who they are, what they want, and how to get it.* Navato, CA: New World Library.

2. Wiseman, L. (2014). *Rookie smarts: Why learning beats knowing in the new game of work.* New York: HarperCollins, p. 24.

3

Developing a Perspective

Many argue that the first stage of leadership development is developing a perspective. Leading is complex enough, but without perspective it can be overwhelming. It is not our intention to force a mind-set on you. Today's organizations are in desperate need of fresh perspectives. We merely want to help you think through developing your own. We don't think you will achieve mind-set Nirvana and never have the need to change. But knowing about mind-sets serves an important function.

Global leadership strategist Stephen Rhinesmith defines *mind-set* as "a predisposition to see the world in a particular way...a filter through which we look at the world...a predisposition to perceive and reason in certain ways...a means of simplifying the environment and bringing to each new experience or event a pre-established frame of reference for understanding it."[1] Mind-sets can help you thoughtfully reflect and responsibly act in a timely manner. Or they can result in a vicious cycle of self-defeating behavior.

One of the foremost minds on the subject of management, Henry Mintzberg, and his colleague Jonathan Gosling, more succinctly define *mind-set* as "perspective" and suggest that managerial leaders must have the five mind-sets listed in Table 3.1.

Table 3.1   The Five Mind-Sets of a Manager[2]

Mind-Set	Description of Mind-Set
The reflective mind-set	**Managing self:** These days, what managers desperately need is to stop and think, to step back and reflect thoughtfully on their experiences.
The analytic mind-set	**Managing organizations:** Good analysis provides a language for organizing; it allows people to share an understanding of what is driving their efforts; it provides measures for performance.
The worldly mind-set	**Managing context:** *Worldly* means being experienced in life, in both sophisticated and practical ways. In other words, it means getting into worlds beyond our own—into other people's circumstances, habits, and cultures—to better know one's own world.
The collaborative mind-set	**Managing relationships:** A truly collaborative mind-set does not involve managing people so much as managing the relationships among people, including our own relationships in teams and projects as well as across divisions and alliances.
The action mind-set	**Managing change:** This mind-set is about developing a sensitive awareness of the terrain and of what the team is capable of doing and thereby helping to set and maintain direction and coax everyone along.

The five mind-sets provide a useful framework for reflection on the development of your managerial leader perspectives. "Everything that every effective manager does is sandwiched between action on the ground and reflection in the abstract. Action without reflection is thoughtless; reflection without action is passive. Every manager has to find a way to combine these two mind-sets—to function at the point where reflective thinking meets practical doing," say Mintzberg and Gosling.[3]

A perspective can be something as simple as "Every person deserves a second chance." Although such a statement is not universally true, it can serve as a healthy perspective that informs how you respond to another's failure or the willingness of a subordinate to take risks. One of the more noteworthy studies on perspective was Douglas McGregor's Theory X and Theory Y. McGregor argued that a manager's perspective determines how that person manages. Theory X managers believe that people are basically lazy, unmotivated, and lack ambition, and they therefore need to be kicked in the butt (our term, not McGregor's). Theory Y managers believe that people are motivated, have developmental potential, and have the capacity for taking responsibility but need training, support, and opportunity.[4] McGregor's theory is relevant; for example, your perspective determines whether you will be a micromanager or a manager who empowers.

While mind-sets inform our thinking and behavior, it is also important to understand that guarding, defending, or becoming inseparable from a mind-set can result in stunting future development and growth.

The Concept of Dignity as a Mind-Set

Whether you are leading people older than you, younger than you, or peers, it is important to understand that people are emotional beings. In all of our research, whether in talking to young or older employees, the theme of respect surfaced—the need for respect and the need to be respected. We would like to extend the conversation beyond respect to the concept of dignity. Donna Hicks explains, "Dignity is different from respect. Dignity is a birthright. We have little trouble seeing this when a child is born; there is no question about children's value and worth. If only we could hold on to this truth about human beings as they grow into adults, if only we could continue to feel their value, then it would be so much easier to treat them well and keep them safe from harm. We must treat others as if they matter, as if they are worthy of care and attention."[5]

Dignity is different from respect in that it is not based on how people perform, what they can do for us, or their likability. Dignity is a feeling of inherent value and worth. In Table 3.2, we outline Hicks' 10 essential elements of dignity.

Table 3.2 The 10 Essential Elements of Dignity[6]

Elements of Dignity	Treating Others with Dignity
Acceptance of identity	Approach people as being neither inferior nor superior to you. Give others freedom to express their authentic selves without fear of being negatively judged. Interact without prejudice or bias, accepting the ways in which race, religion, ethnicity, gender, class, sexual orientation, age, and disability may be at the core of other people's identities. Assume that others have integrity.
Inclusion	Make others feel that they belong, whatever the relationship—whether they are in your family, community, organization, or nation.
Safety	Put people at ease at two levels: physically, so they feel safe from bodily harm, and psychologically, so they feel safe from being humiliated. Help them to feel free to speak without fear of retribution.
Acknowledgment	Give people your full attention by listening, hearing, validating, and responding to their concerns, feelings, and experiences.
Recognition	Validate others for their talents, hard work, thoughtfulness, and help. Be generous with praise and show appreciation and gratitude to others for their contributions and ideas.
Fairness	Treat people justly, with equality, and in an even-handed way, according to agreed-on laws and rules. People feel that you have honored their dignity when you treat them without discrimination or injustice.
Benefit of the doubt	Treat people as trustworthy. Start with the premise that others have good motives and are acting with integrity.
Understanding	Believe that what others think matters. Give them a chance to explain and express their points of view. Actively listen in order to understand them.

Independence	Encourage people to act on their own behalf so that they feel in control of their lives and experience a sense of hope and possibility.
Accountability	Take responsibility for your actions. If you have violated the dignity of another person, apologize. Make a commitment to change your hurtful behaviors.

Developing a perspective about how you lead is important; developing the right perspective is your key to greatness. We challenge you to consider acting on an imperative from Hicks: "Don't miss an opportunity to exert the power you have to remind others of who they are; invaluable, priceless, and irreplaceable [as human beings]."[7]

Having completed a round of golf, a retired CEO of a Fortune 100 company was having drinks at the 19th hole with friends. It was not uncommon for a crowd to gather around him. His stories and interpersonal skills made him an easy listen. After being asked numerous questions ranging from acquisitions to his retirement, he was presented with the question "How many people have you fired in your career?" The crowd was on the edge of their seats, waiting for his response, but his mood immediately changed from affability to somberness. He paused and then proceeded to say that when he fired someone, he took it as a personal failure. It was not the answer they expected. The silence was deafening. His perspective defied the assumptions that people have of powerful people. However, he would say his perspective helped him become who he is.

Acting on your perspective comes at a price. Howard Schultz, of Starbucks fame, has the perspective that part-time employees should enjoy health benefits. While Schultz was trying to raise venture capital, potential investors argued that it was unheard of in retail to offer the benefit. They demanded that he take it off the table. He responded by saying such a move would take the soul out of Starbucks. He won that round but was challenged again when he wanted to take Starbucks public.

Again, banks insisted that he drop the benefit and argued that it would adversely impact the initial public offering price. As a result, he shunned Wall Street and chose a bank in the Midwest that placed a value on the perspective. Schultz' perspective was developed when he was 11 years old. He tells a story of sitting at a family dinner when his father announced that he had lost his job. On the heels of his dad's announcement, his mother revealed that she was pregnant. They were without insurance.[8] He committed to himself if he were ever in a position to help others to not be in that situation—he would do something.

Got Perspective?

Know this: As a managerial leader, not only do you have the potential to impact the people you lead in both positive and negative ways, but you also indirectly influence their family members and friends. Developing a perspective can take time and reflection. After reading this book, you will be much better prepared to have the kind of impact that you want to have.

In the next chapter, we will discuss the challenges of putting your perspectives into practice.

Endnotes

1. Rhinesmith, S. H. (1992). Global mindsets for global managers. *Training and Development, 46*, 63–69.

2. Gosling, J., & Mintzberg, H. (2003). The five minds of a manager. *Harvard Business Review, 81*(11), 54–63.

3. Gosling, J., & Mintzberg, H. (2003). The five minds of a manager. *Harvard Business Review, 81*(11), 54–63.

4. McGregor, D. (2006). *The human side of enterprise.* New York: McGraw-Hill.

5. Hicks, D. (2011). *Dignity: Its essential role in resolving conflict.* London: Yale Press, p. 4.

6. Hicks, D. (2011). *Dignity: Its essential role in resolving conflict.* London: Yale Press, pp. 25–26.

7. Hicks, D. (2011). *Dignity: Its essential role in resolving conflict.* London: Yale Press, p. 3.

8. Schultz, H., & Yang, D. J. (1997). *Pour your heart into it: How Starbucks built a company one cup at a time.* New York: Hyperion.

4

Be True to You

"To attract followers a leader has to be many things to many people. The trick is to pull that off while remaining true to yourself."

—Rob Goffee and Gareth Jones

This may be a chapter you read over and over. It's not that this chapter is difficult to understand. Rather, the research reported here will be helpful to you as you negotiate future career promotions.

Almost every keynote or training event we do is followed by a question-and-answer (Q&A) period. It is through Q&A that we find ourselves being led into further research. Recently, a Baby Boomer manager was concerned that one of his Millennial managers was too hard on his direct reports (who were also Millennials). The Baby Boomer asked, "What's that all about?"

One explanation is that Millennial managers perceive other Millennials much the same way that other managers perceive them; managers of all ages share many of the frustrations. We will go as far as to say that Millennial managers may be a little more critical of other members of their own age cohort than the managers in our prior studies.

Another possibility is that Millennial managers mimic senior managers as a means of distancing themselves from how Millennials are perceived. The behavior can be off-putting to the people they manage (who are likely former peers) and can appear strange to their bosses.

The Desire to Please Your Boss

Obviously, the desire to please your boss is a good thing, but it could mutate into a weakness. When we were doing research for our first book, we found that about 1 in 5 Millennials are very comfortable initiating relationships with authority figures. The ability to initiate a conversation is a skill that allows many Millennials to stand out among their peers to management. If you think about it, it is easier to trust people with whom we can communicate than it is to trust those with whom we cannot. Therefore, when it comes to promoting someone, his or her ability to communicate plays a huge role in the decision. In no way are we downplaying technical skills or know-how; we are just emphasizing the importance of the ability to relate. Odds are if you are being scouted for or already promoted to management, you are not only highly skilled and technically smart but also comfortable with engaging authority figures. Your ability to build a relationship with peers and people older than you is an incredible asset. Once you have turned the heads of management, though, you may be in for one of the most challenging stages of your management career: finding your own identity as a manager and being true to yourself.

One of the more trying results of getting promoted into management is negotiating the tension between the desires to please the person who promoted you while still remaining true to yourself. The tension is normal, and the fact that you feel it is probably indicative of why you were promoted. A key to being true to yourself is having the ability to differentiate from your manager and peers in a healthy way. Sociologist Edwin Friedman defines differentiation as "the capacity of a family member to define his or her own life's goals and values apart from the surrounding togetherness pressures, to say 'I' when others are demanding 'you' and 'we.' It includes the capacity to take maximum responsibility for one's own destiny and well-being."[1]

Friedman outlines the primary characteristics of a well-differentiated person:[2]

1. I have a sense of my own limits and the limits of others.

   ■ A clear understanding of where I end and somebody else begins

   ■ Respect for the rights of others to be the way they are but refusing to let others intrude on my right to be the way I am

2. I have clarity about what I believe.

   ■ What am I certain about and what am I not so certain about

3. I have the courage to take a stand.

   ■ Being clear where I stand even in the face of disapproval

   ■ Capacity to stand firm in the face of strong reactions

4. I have the ability to stay on course.

   ■ Resolve to pursue a goal in the face of sabotage

5. I stay connected.

   ■ Resisting the impulse to attack or cut-off from those that are most reactive to me

Well-differentiated people recognize their dependence on their manager, but they rarely get reactionary in the face of disagreement, critical feedback, or even rejection. They are able to properly identify their emotions, self-manage, and reflect on the broader context of what is happening. Conversely, those who exemplify poor differentiation are so heavily dependent on the acceptance and approval of their managers that they quickly adapt what they think, say, and do in an effort to please the manager. The slang behavioral diagnosis is *brown nose*.

When you become a manager, there are two powerful and typically opposing forces—the forces for togetherness (with both your boss and your peers) and the forces for separateness (for being your own person). Let's begin with the pressure we feel to agree with our superiors. Many young leaders use words like these to explain the tension of differentiation: "When it comes to having to make a difficult decision, it is like I have my boss on one shoulder and the manager I desire to be on the other. I don't want to disappoint the voice of my boss, but I also don't care to be someone I am not." The two figures do not always have to be in conflict, but the inner dialogue can create enough stress to make you want to give up your managerial responsibility. Unfortunately, the inner tension can cause you to make decisions that are not true to you or believable to anyone else. We are not suggesting that you cease to use your boss as a sounding board or that you go rogue. It is always wise to ask yourself, "What would my manager do?" But when your inner voice is drowned out by the fear of disappointing your boss, you risk not being true to yourself or expressing your own voice.

Don't get caught in the trap of always thinking you need to prove yourself. Warren Bennis offers a simple but profound observation about leadership in *On Becoming a Leader*: "Leaders don't set out to be leaders per se, but rather to express themselves fully and freely. Instead of having an interest in proving themselves, leaders have an abiding interest in expressing themselves. The difference is crucial because it is the difference between being driven, as too many people are today, and leading, as too few people do today."[3] In other words, when you cease to express yourself, you cease to lead. Also, when you stop expressing your own voice, you run the risk of being perceived as inauthentic. Every once in a while, ask yourself, "Am I trying to prove something to my boss, or am I trying to express myself?" We in no way want to be dismissive of the value of presenting your credentials. There is a certain amount of "proving" that needs to be done early in your career, but if you get stuck there, you will never achieve your potential.

It Is Inevitable That You Will Have a Disagreement with Your Manager

Okay, give yourself a break. No matter how awesome you are, eventually your manager is going to disagree with or dislike a decision you make. It is simply the natural order of things. If you put all of your energy into avoiding that fateful day, you run the risk of delaying your own development or expressing your own voice. History is littered with stories of students earning their rite of passage by being able to carve out an identity different from that of their teacher. Exercising your own voice can be very threatening because the process can strain or even sever the relationship between you and your manager or mentor.

Our research suggests that Millennials are very concerned about having a good relationship with authority figures—so much so that the details in a disagreement often get lost. Fearing the loss of the relationship takes over. The journey of knowing where you begin and your boss ends starts with being emotionally comfortable with disagreement.

Brace yourself. When you begin to get comfortable with disagreement, your boss or mentor may sense a change in the relationship with you. Studies on healthy mentoring relationships even have a name for it—the *separation phase*. The separation can be characterized by inner turmoil, anxiety, and feelings of loss. At the same time, the separation can be a catalyst for experiencing independence and autonomy.[4] When a person feels less needed by you, consciously or subconsciously, she or he may work to sabotage your ability to be separate from them. You may be told things like, "You are not ready for the next level," "You would not be here without my help," or "You have changed." As challenging as it may be, resist defending yourself or striking back. Though painful, a disagreement with someone you admire and respect can be positive—a sign that you are becoming self-differentiated and expressing your authentic self.

Ultimately you will reach the *redefinition stage*, where your relationship with the mentor is redefined to be more peer-like, and you both are able to express appreciation and gratitude for one another.[5]

The fear of having a disagreement with a boss creates anxiety, but when it comes to peer relationships, the forces for togetherness are even greater. The fear of alienating friends you manage can also be a liability to your development and effectiveness.

It Is Inevitable That Your Relationships with Peers Will Change When You Move into Management

Accept it now. You were perceived as being different the minute you got promoted. One of the interview questions for our book was, "What was the hardest thing about transitioning into management?" The responses were overwhelmingly weighted toward a perceived change in relational dynamics with peers. Many young managers reported a sense of loss and loneliness when they moved into their new role. Some ceased to be invited to lunch or hang out after hours. Others talked about being told, "You are one of them now." One person we interviewed was distraught when she discovered being *unfriended* on Facebook. Here are a few verbatim remarks in response to the question we asked regarding the difficulty of transitioning into management:

> "The most difficult aspect of transitioning into management was getting respect from my former peers."

> "Getting the employees that I used to be on the same level with to see me as a superior instead of just a friend like before."

> "Managing the balance of friendship with professionalism."

> "People I was friends with wouldn't listen to me when I told them to do something."

> "Going from the same level and being friends to now I am in charge of you for business."

> "People who were my former co-workers didn't want to take orders or direction from me."

> "Making my coworkers understand that we were still friends but I was now their boss."

The fact is that most young managers struggle with not being one of the "team" anymore and simultaneously not feeling like a peer with other managers at their level. The good news is that the *tweener* feeling will not last forever. Understanding how to negotiate the transition will make all the difference in the world in how quickly and successfully you move through the stage.

In addition to having a fear of disappointing your manager, more than likely you will also experience a fear of losing your friendships at work. Alert! It can be more difficult to self-differentiate from your friends at work than from your boss. The people with whom you used to commiserate, dream, and break the rules are the same people you will ultimately have to hold accountable. And, by the way, holding them accountable was a top-five challenge with managing peers. A successful transition to management will require you to have the ability to be separate from friends at work without losing connection with them. Being separate does not mean that you are better than or that you no longer care about them. One interviewee put it this way: "I think the hardest thing I have ever done is get my coworkers to understand that we were still friends but I was now their boss." The caring part is what fuels your ability to stay connected in the face of criticism or even sabotage. Again, be prepared to hear statements intended to sabotage your separateness, such as "You are not the same," "You have changed," "You are full of yourself," or "You are a brown nose." And brace yourself for the next section.

The People Who Care About Us the Most Are the Ones Who Most Likely Will Hold Us Back

Seriously, our enemies are far less effective at sabotaging us than our friends. We know of a promising graduate student who had the privilege of studying under a leading consultant. The consultant specialized in consulting for nonprofits. The professor was so taken by the abilities of his student that he started using her on some of his consultations. It was not long until the student was securing clients of her own. She eventually ventured outside the boundaries of the nonprofit world and started tending to clients like Microsoft. Her professor voiced his disappointment by telling her that he trained her to work in nonprofits, not corporate America. Her decision led to a strain in the relationship, but she had to follow her own path.

As weird as it sounds, it is generally not the people who are against us who hold us back in life. It is often the people who are most invested in us. Ironically, key relationships can become threatened when you start exploring your own path. This is true when it comes to relationships with parents, mentors, and bosses. It's not always true, but many times these important people in our lives feel threatened in some way by our independence. We are not suggesting that you cease to listen to people you respect or you believe to have your best interest in mind. Just be prepared to experience the inner conflict that comes with exploring your own voice. The threat of losing support or sponsorship from an authority figure can be daunting. You have to think long term and not short term. In the short term, you may second-guess yourself or be tempted to acquiesce to what got you where you are now, but it could adversely affect your ability to get where you want to go.

Organizations by Nature Exert a Powerful Force Against Self-Differentiation

For centuries, leaders have made bad decisions that were not in concert with their values or what they believed. Although there were clearly a few rotten eggs, most members of the leadership at Enron didn't begin their careers with the intention of destroying the lives of innocent employees, cheating investors, or undermining the public's confidence. Perhaps for a myriad of reasons, these people just could not resist the gravitational pull from the organization because once they got inside, it had more influence over them than they had over it.

There is a reason national political candidates try to present themselves as Washington outsiders. Has anyone ever run an election campaign based on being a Washington insider? Well, maybe. However, politicians who wish to be recognized as agents of change promote the perception that their views have not been influenced by the establishment. Innately, we resonate with the idea that real change comes from the outside. However, we are resigned to the fact that once a leader drinks the water in Washington, he or she becomes a pawn in the system. The skepticism is warranted but should not be limited to big nasty corporations and politicians. Religious, educational, and nonprofit institutions have exerted the same kind of force over their leaders. Ronald Heifetz explains, "A leader earns influence by adjusting to the expectation of followers."[6]

It is not uncommon for the founder of a thriving business to take it public and then find that she has less control over the company than it had over her. Ultimately, her founding principles will meet with challenge, and she will have to give in, step down, or get out.

Again, the forces for togetherness can undermine anyone who seeks to self-differentiate (be separate). While it is easy to moralize the outcomes of poor differentiation, our point is for you to be aware that organizations can have greater power over you than you have over yourself.

Edwin Friedman argues that self-differentiation, if not the definition of leadership, is the key to leadership. True leaders are willing to challenge the status quo, risk being on the outside, and stick to their values.

Without the ability to self-differentiate, it is impossible to manage intense or complex relationships. It is far easier said than done, but learning how to self-differentiate does not happen overnight. Professionally speaking, for many, it is a process that unfolds over early and middle career development. For some, it may never happen, and they may be destined for a life of reacting to everyone and everything around them; being a great leader is not in their future.

Being true to one's self is key to being true to others. In the next chapter, we will discuss the importance of being authentic.

Endnotes

1. Friedman, E. H. (1985). *Generation to Generation: Family Process in Church and Synagogue.* New York: Guilford Press, p. 27.

2. Friedman, E. (Producer), & Dawkins Productions. (Director). (2007). *Reinventing leadership* [DVD]. (Available Guilford Press, 370 Seventh Avenue, New York, NY 10001.) Notes retrieved from https://www.emu.edu/seminary/timothy/documents/FiveCharacteristics.pdf.

3. Bennis, W. G. (1991). *On Becoming a Leader.* Reading, MA: Addison-Wesley.

4. Kram, K. E. (1983). Phases of the mentor relationship. *Academy of Management Journal, 26*(4), 608–625.

5. Kram, K. E. (1983). Phases of the mentor relationship. *Academy of Management Journal, 26*(4), 608–625.

6. Heifetz, R. (1994). *Leadership without Easy Answers.* Cambridge: Harvard University Press, p. 17.

5

Be True to Others

"Engaging authentically with people is the first task of genuine leadership."

—Margie Worrell

Authenticity is not an innate quality—that is, you are not born with it. Second, being an authentic leader is not something you can say about yourself; it must be attributed to you.[1] Some believe that to be authentic, you have to present yourself the same way in every situation. At first thought, this notion seems reasonable, but when you really think about it—not so much. The way you interact with your boss is not the same way you need to interact with your family, peers, team members, or clients. It is not only okay to present yourself differently in various situations but crucial to being perceived as authentic.

It's Okay to Identify with People Your Age

There is nothing more restrictive than feeling that you cannot be you. In Chapter 2, "Making the Transition into Management," we reported that the most positive thing about Millennial managers is that Millennial employees can relate to them. Don't give up one of the best things you have going for you as a young manager because you think you have to present yourself the same way to your age cohort as you would to your manager.

It's Okay to Identify with People Older Than You

In the same sense, don't try to downplay the opportunities you have to connect with other managers and executives in your organization for the sake of saving face with your peers. Don't apologize for the level of conversation to which you have access. Don't allow your enthusiasm and energy for either context to be muted.

What Does It Mean to Be Authentic?

Herminia Ibarra argues that having too rigid a definition of authenticity can get in the way of effective leadership. She succinctly captures the challenge of presenting our authentic self: "Many of us work with people who don't share our cultural norms and have different expectations for how we should behave. It can often seem as if we have to choose between what is expected—and therefore effective—and what feels authentic."[2] Negotiating the space flanked by what is expected and what feels authentic is the Millennial manager's world.

Rob Goffee and Gareth Jones wrote a great piece titled "Managing Authenticity." In it, they argue that establishing authenticity as a leader is a two-part challenge: "First, you have to ensure that your words are consistent with your deeds; otherwise, followers will never accept you as authentic. The second challenge of authentic leadership is finding common ground with the people you seek to recruit as followers. This means you will have to present different faces to different audiences, a requirement that many people find hard to square with authenticity."[3]

Goffee and Jones suggest that there are things you can consciously do to help others perceive you as being an authentic leader. Management literature calls this *impression management*.[4] However, keep in mind that attempting to manage how people perceive you without being authentic can come off as very inauthentic and can lead to a loss of credibility. Goffee and Jones say that learning about yourself is foundational to managing your authenticity and suggest the following activities: explore your biography, return to your roots, avoid comfort zones, and seek out honest feedback. The aforementioned activities are not for the purpose of protecting your identity but for pursuing a better understanding of it. The following sections address each of these activities.

Exploring Your Autobiography

Google the phrase *never forget where you come from*. You will see that it is the mantra of many successful people. If someone admonishes you with such advice, it is a good sign because it means you have already attained a certain level of success.

One of the downsides of upward mobility is forgetting about or distancing yourself from your humble beginnings. A great example of not forgetting where you come from is William Leonard, former president and CEO of Aramark Corporation. Bill is an avid golfer and belongs to several prestigious golf clubs, but he enjoys playing with his friends. His private jet can whisk him off to play anywhere, but you will find him most Saturdays playing with his comrades at a course that is nice but nowhere as prestigious as his others. He has not forgotten where he comes from. You may not be CEO yet, but stay in touch with where you come from, and odds are you will make a great one!

Exploring your past is a reflective adventure in which you revisit the events and people that have most influenced your life. Robert Clinton offers a great framework for thinking about influential people in your life. He argues that growing leaders have four types of mentors in their life: upward, friendship, sandpaper, and downward.[5] He uses the metaphor of a compass to diagram the relationships. Take out a sheet of paper and label north, south, east, and west. At the north point, list all of your *upward mentors*—people who are older than you who have had significant influence in your life. You may list people such as a grandfather, an aunt, a professor, a coach, or an author. In most cases, you probably knew the person but not in all cases. What did you learn from these people that would cause you to hold them in such high esteem?

The mentors on the east side of the compass are called *friendship mentors*. Friendship mentors are persons you grew up with and with whom you advanced through the life stages (i.e., attended school, started career, started family, and so on). They are people you go to for advice. Friendship mentors are often the best sounding boards. Write down your friendship mentors. Don't limit the list to people you speak with frequently. Friendship mentors can go for years without talking, but when they connect, it is like no time has passed.

Let's navigate across the compass to the west. Do you feel the turbulence? You should. Here is where you want to write down the names of *sandpaper mentors*. Sandpaper mentors are people who rub you the wrong way. They have the uncanny ability to find a flaw in whatever you do. They make you feel like you are never good enough. The beauty about a sandpaper mentor is that you don't have to seek them out—they will find you! Reflect on the sandpaper mentors in your life. Are there any themes in what they have said to you? How did you respond to them? What was true about what they had to say to you? Although they are not pleasant, it is important to have sandpaper mentors in your life. We are not suggesting that you weight what they say over what other mentors say (unless you want to be on antidepressants the rest of your life). Try to rise above their abrasiveness and take the opportunity to learn more about yourself.

Finally, at the south point of the compass, write the names of people you are mentoring or who consider you to be their upward mentor. The list could include siblings, nieces, nephews, your own children, or people you teach, coach, or lead. What value does investing in them bring? What are you learning about yourself as a result of investing in the relationship?

We want to encourage you to examine your relationship compass and make the effort to reach out to people you listed (with the exception of the sandpaper mentors) and let them know the role they have played or are playing in your life. You don't want to put pressure on them or you but rather acknowledge the value you place on the relationship.

Returning to Your Roots

Maybe it is just us, but it seems like every movie about a professional who loses her or his way returns to a small hometown, downplays success to satisfy the locals, meets an old flame, and ends up in agriculture or the arts. The theme is popular because there is something transformational about returning to your roots. Living in a highly transient world is exciting, but it can also untether us from things that matter. Listening online to a hometown radio station, attending a reunion, or reconnecting with old friends can be a catalyst for rediscovering ourselves. Going home creates the potential to be taken down a notch, built up beyond merit, or get grounded. It is in the space between that we grapple with our own story and discover our own authenticity.

Avoiding Comfort Zones

Comfort zones insulate us from feeling vulnerable. Yet one of the more lauded attributes people desire to see in a leader is vulnerability. Patrick Lencioni argues that building trust, as a leader, is impossible without the ability to be vulnerable.[6] Vulnerability allows you to connect on a deeper level with people. Be aware that inappropriate disclosure or a lack of contextual awareness can cause attempts at vulnerability to be counterproductive.

You can get out of your comfort zone by reading publications that are not related to your field of expertise. Engage in conversations that force you to examine your own beliefs. If you usually watch Fox News, try MSNBC every once in a while. If you are the person always arguing to cut expenses, make the pitch for ways to spend. Order something new on the menu or be bold enough to change your routine. Habits are hard to give up because they give us a sense of stability.

Adam Kahane, an accomplished strategist for Royal Dutch Shell, speaks of an out-of-the-comfort-zone experience he had while participating in the Mont Fleur Project. The Mont Fleur scenario exercise was undertaken in South Africa during 1991 and 1992, on the heels of Nelson Mandela's release from prison. In the midst of deep conflict, economist Pieter Le Roux, director of the Institute for Social Development at the University of the Western Cape, brought together a diverse group of 22 prominent South Africans—politicians, activists, scholars, and businesspeople from across the ideological spectrum—to develop and disseminate a set of stories about what might happen in their country over the next decade.

Kahane reflects on his experience: "I was struck by the fact that I was more effective on the Mont Fleur project than I had ever been before. Clearly, I had done something right, but I didn't know what it was. Eventually I figured it out. In Mont Fleur, I had almost no time to prepare. With more time, I would have done my normal Shell thing: reading up on the problem, forming opinions, and coming in with a recommendation. I was effective because I arrived in ignorance and respect. I gave up a stance of knowing and arrogance, and replaced it with one of wonder and reverence."[7]

Ibarra warns that getting out of our comfort zones "can make us feel like impostors, because it involves doing things that may not come naturally. But it is outside of our comfort zones that we learn the most about leading effectively."[8] Give yourself permission to go off script.

Seeking feedback can also move us out of our comfort zone.

Seeking Honest Feedback

A colleague of ours frequently asserts, "Feedback is the breakfast of champions." It sounds great if the feedback is steak and eggs. If all of the feedback is positive, it is much easier to digest. The truth is that feedback can be intimidating, demoralizing, and hurtful, and it can leave you with a stomachache. We need all kinds of feedback, but it is tempting to leave the less positive stuff out of our diet.

It is well known that feedback is important to personal and professional growth. But we can still consciously or subconsciously thwart genuine attempts by others to give us feedback as a means of protecting ourselves. We may not even be aware of it, but we self-protect when we become defensive, make excuses, qualify our actions, or project shortcomings onto other people. Self-protecting sends the message that you are not open to feedback. But you don't want to alienate people who want to help you maximize your potential. We trust that you'll be able to spot the people who are not invested in you and are out to undermine your success. In those cases, when they drop a pile of horse crap on you, look around because there has to be a pony nearby.

A safe place to go for feedback is to your upward and friendship mentors. Once you build tolerance and acceptance levels for all kinds of feedback, it becomes easier to put yourself out there to colleagues, clients, and even demanding bosses. We say "build tolerance" because people who seek feedback on their performance more frequently are apt to hear more views that may be difficult to reconcile with their own.[9]

Don't ever stop seeking feedback. Unfortunately, the higher you go in your organization, the more restricted you may feel when it comes to soliciting feedback.[10] It is a sad phenomenon because your openness to feedback should grow with your level of responsibility.

The Challenges of Being Authentic When Transitioning into a New Role

Leadership transitions require us to move out of our comfort zone. Ibarra found that leaders in transition most often grapple with authenticity in the following situations:[11]

- Taking charge in an unfamiliar role
- Selling your ideas (and yourself)

- Processing negative feedback
- Having a playful frame of mind

Beware that the first three challenges listed above can trigger a bad case of *impostor syndrome* (feeling like a fraud). Pauline Clance and Suzanne Imes define the impostor syndrome as, "The psychological experience of believing that one's accomplishments came about not through genuine ability, but as a result of having been lucky, having worked harder than others, or having manipulated other people's impressions."[12] Clance and Imes' original study was focused on women executives subjected to stereotype threat, but the theory is generally accepted to apply to the general population. The original study is highly applicable to Millennial managers in that both women and Millenials are highly subject to stereotype threat. The threat women faced was being perceived as being less capable than men. The threat Millennials face is being perceived as being less capable than people older than them. The good news is that people who suffer from the impostor syndrome are usually high-achievers and don't suffer from low self-esteem. You may struggle with the impostor syndrome if you:[13]

- Fear people are going to expose you for a fraud
- Minimize the compliments of others
- Attribute your success to luck
- Worry about not being able to repeat your successes
- Dread evaluation
- Feel less capable than your peers

The impostor syndrome is normal but can transmute into maladaptive behavior—like being inauthentic for the sake of masking your insecurities. Overcoming the impostor syndrome requires shifting evaluation from others to the self; for instance, "Did I put forth my best effort on getting the Starbucks account?" or "Did I do the right thing?." Ultimately, recognize your self-worth is not based on what you do but on who you are as a person. Work on becoming less dependent upon the affirmation of others (see Chapter 4, "Be True to You").

As for having a playful frame of mind, Millennials by-and-large do not have a problem with that. Playfulness among other things is characterized as the willingness to try something new, experiment, and be curious. You come plug-and-play—please don't lose it!

You Have to Be Believed to Be Heard

Before you will be convincing, you have to first be convinced. We use the term *convinced* because we believe this term to be the essence of our ability to influence. Many strategic initiatives (e.g., empowerment on the frontline, diversity in the corporate boardroom, abolition of sexual harassment around the water cooler, and so on) have had minimal or no impact due to unconvincing leadership. If a leader is not convinced of something, he or she will not be effective in influencing the target group. Leaders who try to convince others to embrace an idea of which they themselves are not convinced lose credibility. Being incredulous renders a leader unbelievable, thus jeopardizing future influence attempts. In his book *You've Got to Be Believed to Be Heard*, Bert Decker asserts, "If you don't believe in someone on an emotional level, little if any of what they have to say will get through."[14] If you are not convinced of who you are in each relational context (peers, subordinates, or superiors), how can anybody else be?

In the next chapter, we will further explore the concept of a generation and its impact upon relating in the workplace.

Endnotes

1. Goffee, R., & Jones, G. (2005). Managing authenticity. *Harvard Business Review, 83*(12), 87–94.

2. Ibarra, H. (2015). The authenticity paradox. *Harvard Business Review, 93*(1/2), 52–59.

3. Goffee, R., & Jones, G. (2005). Managing authenticity. *Harvard Business Review, 83*(12), 87–94.

4. Goffman, E. (1959). *The Presentation of Self in Everyday Life.* New York: Anchor/Doubleday.

5. Clinton, R. J. (1996). Phases of leadership development. Lecture, Master's course at Southern California College.

6. Lencioni, P. (2002). *The Five Dysfunctions of a Team: A Leadership Fable.* San Francisco: Jossey-Bass.

7. Senge, P. M. (1999). *The Dance of Change: The Challenges of Sustaining Momentum in Learning Organizations.* New York: Currency/Doubleday.

8. Ibarra, H. (2015). The authenticity paradox. *Harvard Business Review, 93*(1/2), 52–59, p. 55.

9. Stobbeleir, K., Ashford, S., & Buyens, D. (2011). Self-regulation of creativity at work: The role of feedback-seeking behavior in creative performance. *Academy of Management Review, 54*(4), 811–831.

10. van der Rijt, J., Van den Bosch, P., & Segers, M. S. R. (2013). Understanding informal feedback seeking in the workplace. *European Journal of Training and Development, 37*(1), 72–85. doi:http://dx.doi.org/10.1108/03090591311293293.

11. Ibarra, H. (2015). The authenticity paradox. *Harvard Business Review, 93*(1/2), 52–59.

12. Clance, P., & Imes, S. (1978). The impostor phenomenon in high achieving women: Dynamics and therapeutic intervention. *Psychotherapy: Theory, Research, and Practice,* 15, 241–247.

13. Langford, J., & Clance, P. (1993). The impostor phenomenon: Recent research finding regarding dynamics, personality, and family patterns. *Psychotherapy: Theory, Research, and Practice, 30*(3), 495–501.

14. Decker, B. (1993). *You've Got to Be Believed to Be Heard.* New York: St. Martin's Press.

6

Generational Differences: Fact or Fiction?

I f you manage a team, odds are that you have faced the difficulties of managing multiple generations. Seventy-five percent of the managers in a survey conducted recently by Ernst & Young agree that "managing multi-generational teams is a challenge."[1] You might even have experienced some fairly strong feelings on the topic yourself. The odds are also good that you have been bombarded with all kinds of advice for how to manage your team. The media is full of horror stories, opinions, "true stories," and even...survey results.

Despite the buzz, however, some critics say that the issue is not worthy of attention. In this chapter, we show why it is, and we review two perspectives[2] from the social sciences—the maturational and life course perspectives—to explain why Millennials, Xers, and Baby Boomers bring different values and expectations to the workplace.

The Maturational Perspective

We frequently hear that the current generation gap is simply the result of a new group of young people challenging authority, rethinking the status quo, and experimenting with different lifestyles, as all groups do when they enter adulthood. It is natural to wonder if generational differences really exist or whether all the noise is just part of a stage that each cohort goes through when it's their turn to enter the workforce. After all, the Baby Boomers shook things up during their early years but are now known for their corporate loyalty.

The idea that everyone has similar experiences and expresses the same views, moods, and attitudes during the same life stage is known as the *maturational perspective*, or sometimes *maturational theory*. The maturational perspective views biological development as the major determinant of behavior. According to this perspective, people's values, attitudes, goals, preferences, and abilities change as a function of age. Crawling, walking, and speaking are all normative at specific stages of early development. A six-year-old has the coordination and balance to ride a bicycle, but a two-year-old does not. In the same way, attitudes and values emerge, as appropriate, at each life stage.

According to this view, it's normal to defy authority and experiment with alternative lifestyles during early adulthood. Expressing dissatisfaction with the status quo is normative at this stage. In his 1995 book *Managing Generation X*,[3] Bruce Tulgan lists a number of behaviors and attitudes that sound a lot like what people are saying about Millennials today. According to Tulgan, Xers were characterized in the mainstream media as "sullen and contemptuous," "impetuous," "naïve," "arrogant," "short on attention," and "materialistic."[4] There were no "Managing Generation Baby Boom" books written in the 1970s, but the media from the period was full of similar descriptions of Baby Boomers.[5] As we show in the next chapter, the image of Generation X has changed significantly over the last 20 years. It's easy to conclude, then, that each cohort simply goes through a maturationally determined "awkward stage" as they emerge into adulthood. The life course perspective provides a richer understanding.

The Life Course Perspective

The life course perspective is more comprehensive than the maturational perspective. It evolved from cohort theory, also called generational theory, and extends it with a multidisciplinary approach to human development. In life course theory, demographers, historians, developmental psychologists, and sociologists look for the interactions between sociological phenomena and developmental processes. According to cohort theory, our worldview is heavily influenced by significant events that occur during our teens and 20s. Macro-scale events create experiences shared by most individuals within an age group and form the basis of common outlook and shared values, attitudes, and beliefs.[6] People who experience a sociological context at the same point in their psychosocial development are likely to forge a common perspective or mind-set that stays with them throughout their entire life.

One obvious example of a major event that left an imprint on an entire generation is the Great Recession of 2008. Clearly people of all ages were impacted by the banking crisis and the stock market crash that precipitated the recession. Many people in or near retirement lost significant portions of their retirement savings, and workers of all ages lost jobs. Major banks and car manufacturers came close to collapse, and there was widespread fear that the economy was heading toward a depression similar to the Great Depression of the 1930s. People who were finishing school during this recession and entering the economy were unable to find jobs. The jobs that they did find tended overwhelmingly to be low-paying and underutilized the skills they had developed. This experience has left Millennials with a sense of diminished expectations. As a consequence, they tend to buy smaller cars and houses—if they buy at all—and to place greater emphasis on savings than did Boomers or Xers at the same age.[7] Their financial habits resemble those of the Silent generation who survived the Great Depression 80 years ago. They are skeptical of financial advisors, and despite their smaller incomes, Millennials on average have a savings rate nearly as high as those of Boomers and Xers.[8] However, unlike the Silents, Millennials are optimistic about the future and expect the economy to return to a state of rapid growth.

Additional examples of historical events that had powerful cohort effects are World War II, the Cold War, the Space Race, the Beatles, the civil rights movement and the Kennedy and King assassinations, the Vietnam War, the sexual revolution, the women's liberation movement,

Watergate, the fall of the Berlin Wall, the explosion of the *Columbia* space shuttle, the Columbine massacre, 9/11, the rise of the Internet, and the dot-com boom and bust. All of these events are social markers that frame life experience and shape values, beliefs, and attitudes. The transition to delivery drones, self-driving cars, wearable computing, and continuous data collection will likely have a major impact on the worldview of the next generation.

We don't really know the younger Millennials yet, in cultural terms. The youngest Millennials are just turning 15 this year. We expect that they will share many of the imprints of their older cohort-mates. But the younger ones have 10 or more years to go before their attitudes and outlook have solidified. We have no way of knowing what major events or crises might occur in the next decade. The number of possibilities is infinite. Perhaps the rising level of racially motivated violence in the United States will galvanize the younger Millennials into a 2030s reprise of the civil rights movement. We can't guess what form the movement might take, only that it will be a reflection of the times in which it takes place. No doubt some communications technology such as social media or wearable streaming devices will play a significant role, unlike the original Civil Rights movement of the 1960s.

Generational Subcultures

Life course theory can be extended by thinking of generations as distinct subcultures. To an anthropologist, a culture is more than just the language, art, cuisine, and festivals of an ethnic group. Each culture has its own set of assumptions about the universe, as well as values and beliefs about how life and the world work. For an anthropologist, these are the things that distinguish one group from another. The celebrations, rituals, art, and language are reflections of the deeper meanings shared by members of the group.

In his Organizational Behavior class, Joel likes to show his students a photograph of a three-year-old boy sitting in a plastic tub, scrubbing a snake that could easily swallow him. The picture was taken in Cambodia or Thailand and can be found in various places on the Internet. The snake is a python that could very well have been more than 10 feet long at the time the picture was taken.

There are gasps and snorts from the class when they see the picture. Obviously, part of the reaction is based on the fact that the python is a formidable predator, capable of swallowing antelopes and even crocodiles. Some students question the parents' judgment. The image clearly challenges our assumptions and attitudes about snakes. In Western culture, we see snakes as evil. In the biblical book of Genesis, Adam and Eve are tricked by a snake into disobeying God. We have no positive imagery of snakes. There are no traditional stories in which the hero is a snake. When we do consider snakes, it is to warn other hikers of rattlers on the trail or provide "fun facts" about how quickly the bite of a water moccasin can kill a person.

If you are a Millennial and your parents are Baby Boomers, the idea that you belong to a different culture from them might seem strange at first. Obviously, you share your parents' ethnic background. However, there is no rule that says a person can belong to only a single culture.

Suppose that you grew up in the United States, but your parents emigrated from Taiwan. They speak Mandarin, and most of their friends are Chinese—many of them also born overseas. You eat mooncakes with your parents, grandparents, and their friends at Chinese New Year. So which culture do you belong to—American or Taiwanese? Both.

It is not much of a stretch, then, if we follow the anthropologists' definition, to say that people who grew up in a specific period share an understanding of the world and a way of relating to it and to each other that is different than for others born in the same place 20 or 40 years earlier. Culture is a system of shared meaning. As we show below, each generation has its own system of shared meanings, resulting from its time and place in history and the critical events that impressed themselves on the psyche of those who were coming of age when those events occurred.

Defining the Generations

In the remainder of this chapter, we summarize the differences between the Baby Boom, X, and Millennial generations. These three generations comprised over 95% of the workforce in the United States as of 2014. We also provide a brief description of the Silent generation, which constituted the remaining 5%.

There is no precise definition for the generational cohorts. Demographers define the Baby Boom generation to include anyone born between 1946 and 1964, Generation X as people born between 1965 and 1977, and Millennials as those born between 1978 and 1999. These years correspond to changes in the birthrate. They do not take into account the shared beliefs and attitudes of the people born in those years.

We use a different approach. We are interested in understanding how different groups of people think and behave. We want to know which groups share attitudes based on a shared belief about how the world works. The demographers' birth year groupings are close to ours, but they don't quite fit our definition. Following Ron Zemke, Claire Raines, and Bob Filipczak, we use the years 1943–1960 for Boomers, 1961–1980 for Generation X, and 1981–2000 for Millennials.[9]

We offer a brief overview of the events that shaped the cultures of the different generations. There are a number of books that do a very nice job of getting even more deeply into this. For excellent descriptions of the world that shaped each of the generations, see *Generations, Inc.* by Meagan Johnson and Larry Johnson[10] or *Generations at Work* by Zemke, Raines, and Filipczak.[11] For a very detailed and entertaining description, see *Generations* by William Strauss and Neil Howe,[12] who published their book in 1991, the same year that Doug Coupland's book *Generation X* came out. Strauss and Howe call Xers "13ers," in reference to the fact that they are the thirteenth generation of citizens of the United States. Despite this, Strauss and Howe provide an insightful and accurate description of the group we now refer to as Generation X.

The Silent Generation

The Silent generation (also called the Traditionalist, Veteran, or Builder generation[13]) is the smallest generation of the past 125 years, with roughly 20 million people alive today who were born between 1925 and 1942. Silents now make up roughly 5% of the workforce in the United States, and so we devote somewhat less attention to them in this book than we do to the other generations.

Unlike the Baby Boom, X, and Millennial generations, as well as those that came before, the Silent generation did not create dramatic upheavals when they came of age. There were no riots or demonstrations on campus. Nor were there angry or bemused members of older generations. Instead, Silents entered the workforce doing their best to emulate their elders. Their failure to make the kind of noise expected of a young cohort earned them the mocking nickname the Silent generation.

They grew up during the Depression, when unemployment in the United States exceeded 25%, and they were therefore grateful for their jobs. Their ethos was to work within the system rather than to change it. Their loyalty to their employers dominated the work environment until the 1970s.

It seems fair to say that the Silent generation valued not making waves while at the same time valuing authenticity. Even though they did their best to fit in at college and work, they were nonetheless known as nonconformists. The Beat Generation of the 1950s emphasized nonconformity, exploration of Eastern religions, spiritual and artistic expression, and rejection of materialism. Andy Warhol's famous tomato soup can paintings were an example of the anti-materialist Beat sentiment. The Beat culture later became the genesis for the counterculture movement of the 1960s.

The Silent label was applied prematurely. Elvis Presley, Chuck Berry, Ray Charles, Buddy Holly, Little Richard, James Brown, Smokey Robinson, Roy Orbison, Bob Dylan, and the Beatles were all from the so-called

Silent generation. Without them, of course, there would be no rock and roll.

Similarly, without the Silent generation, we would not have had the civil rights movement. The Silent generation produced almost every major figure of the civil rights movement, including Martin Luther King, Jr., Malcolm X, and Cesar Chavez. Vaclav Havel, writer, leader of the Velvet Revolution, and first president of the Czech Republic, was also a Silent.

Perhaps because of their patriotism, members of the Silent generation waited until after the dire business of World War II was complete before making their noise.

Baby Boomers

Baby Boomers are primarily the children of members of the Silent generation who fought in World War II. The war prevented young families from getting started, but when the soldiers returned from the war, they settled down and began having children.

During the war, almost all industry had been directed toward the war effort. Food, clothing, and automobile manufacturers had all been enlisted to help defeat the Nazis in Europe and Imperial Japan in Asia. With the end of the war in 1945, all of these industries reverted to civilian manufacture.

Civilians had forgone all but the most essential consumption so that all available resources could be used to help win the war. Fabric was reserved for uniforms, tents, and other military applications. The same was also true of most basic materials. This created a huge unmet demand for goods that skyrocketed as soon as the war was over. In addition, all of the new families that were just starting out needed cribs, furniture, lawn mowers, kitchen appliances, and cars. The economy grew rapidly as manufacturers expanded production to meet this new demand.

The GI Bill made it easier for couples to buy homes, further fueling the economic expansion. Home ownership in the United States jumped from under 44% in 1940 to 62% in 1960. Most of this growth took place in the new suburbs. As home ownership for new families soared, so did the birth rate.

Baby Boomers were raised during a time when the economy was expanding. They were raised with permissiveness, as prescribed by Dr. Benjamin Spock, many by stay-at-home moms whose full-time homemaker status was made possible by the booming economy. *Dr. Spock's Baby and Child Care* was published in 1946.[14] Spock's advice was revolutionary. Instead of following the prevailing opinion of the time, which was that emotions and affection should be withheld from children in order to avoid spoiling them, Spock advocated emotional openness and authenticity. He encouraged parents to express affection toward their children and to trust their own judgment rather than listen to the so-called experts.

The oldest Boomers were in their teens when *Sputnik* was launched and the Space Race began. They were just entering their 20s at the start of the Vietnam War and the free speech movement.

Boomers were raised by parents who valued their jobs and shared their work ethic with their children. Silent generation parents had experienced life without work, and it was painful. Baby Boomers came of age at a time when demand for labor was high: Jobs were plentiful, and employers took care of employees. Employers might not have been motivated by a benevolent philosophy (some were), but it was in their interest to act as if they did. Boomers came of age in a time of plenty and were taught the importance of a solid work ethic, they witnessed the rebuilding of Europe following the devastation of WWII and the beginning of space flight, and they were fully aware of the ravages of polio and measles and also their near eradication. It should therefore not be surprising that Boomers expected to be able to accomplish pretty much anything if they put in effort. Having been raised according to the self-esteem-building teachings of Dr. Spock only enhanced the world-changing optimism of this generation.

Finally, Boomers were socialized to, uh, socialize. Membership in social clubs, fraternities, and sororities grew during the 1950s and were an important focus for social life through the 1960s. It was a time when parents taught their children "It's not what you know, it's who you know."

Generation Xers

Xers grew up during a less optimistic time. The first Xers were born at the height of the Cold War. In 1962, the Cuban Missile Crisis brought the world dangerously close to nuclear destruction. The following year, John F. Kennedy was assassinated. The assassinations of Martin Luther King, Jr., and Robert Kennedy followed shortly. The Vietnam War escalated, claiming the lives of nearly 60,000 U.S. military personnel. In 1974, President Nixon was forced to resign for his role in the Watergate scandal, and the OPEC oil embargo caused gasoline prices to quadruple. Long before YouTube, television crews filmed fistfights in gas station lines and carried stories of people cheating on the new rationing schemes. It was at this time that the Honda Civic was first sold in the United States.

Businesses downsized, either in response to worsening economic conditions or in the wake of leveraged buyouts. Many Xers saw their parents lose jobs with companies to which they had been loyal. It didn't matter that the parents had worked late many nights to make sure a project was completed on time. Xers' worldview, therefore, is that employers cannot be counted on. Loyalty does not buy job security. In fact, one should expect that the company one works for will be chewed up and spit out in a leveraged buyout or bought out just to take the competition off the market: It's nothing personal, just business.

Xers were often referred to as "latchkey kids." As children, they often came home from school to empty houses. The divorce rate in the United States surged in the 1970s, and many children grew up in single-parent households. Married women were also working, either out of economic necessity or because they were exercising the newfound freedom for women to enjoy a career of their own.

As a consequence, Gen Xers seek closeness from friends and surrogate "tribal" families. The TV sitcoms *Friends* and *How I Met Your Mother* are two well-known examples. In both series, many of the parents are either absent or too self-involved to provide the kind of emotional support and closeness the main characters get from one another.

Xers entered the workforce during a period of high inflation and poor job prospects. In the words of Doug Coupland, from whose novel Generation X gets its name, the only jobs available were "McJobs." Coupland refers to the general feeling about their prospects of young adults as "lessness."[15]

The 1970s brought a steep decline in the economic welfare of children. By 1990, roughly 20% of Xers lived in poverty. Traditionally, the age bracket with the highest poverty rate were people over age 65. However, because of changes in public policy and the skyrocketing divorce rate, the age bracket with the highest poverty rate shifted abruptly.

This distinction followed Xers into their 20s. Whereas in 1967, male 20-something Boomer wage earners took home 74% as much as older males, in 1988 Xers were earning only 54% as much as older males. Between 1973 and 1988, the median income of households headed by someone under 25 fell by 18% (adjusted for inflation and family size).

Because of these conditions, Xers view work as transactional. Work is for earning money, not for forming emotional attachments.

Millennials

Millennials grew up in very different circumstances than Generation Xers. Most parents of Millennials are younger Boomers and older Xers who vowed that their children would not grow up as latchkey children. Although they typically work as much as, or even more than, their parents did, parents of Millennials found ways to spend more time with their children. A study by Garey Ramey and Valerie A. Ramey, economists at the University of California, San Diego, analyzed multiple surveys, conducted by other researchers between 1965 and 2007, on how Americans spend their time. The results show that the amount of time spent on child care has risen dramatically since the mid-1990s. The study found that between 1995 and 2007, the amount of time mothers in the United States spent attending to the needs of their children rose from an average of about 12 hours a week to 21.2 hours a week for college-educated women.[16] Betsey Stevenson and Dan Sacks, economists at the Wharton School of the University of Pennsylvania, also found that college-educated fathers increased the amount of time they spent with their children to 9.6 hours a week, more than double the pre-1995 rate of 4.5 hours. Non-college-educated fathers showed nearly equal gains to 6.8 hours, up from 3.7 hours. The phrase "quality time" came into usage in the mid-1970s, and by the late 1980s or early 1990s, parents were using it to differentiate between time on maintenance activities like getting the kids to brush their teeth and time spent reading together and playing catch in the backyard. During this same period, parents' focus shifted from instilling obedience in their children to engendering friendship and understanding.

While these changes were happening in the parenting sphere, the self-esteem movement that started with Benjamin Spock took hold in the educational and youth sports systems. Elementary school curricula began to emphasize self-esteem in the 1980s. Sports programs, which had previously been highly competitive, became inclusive. Trophies were awarded for participation as well as achievement. Although teachers are still authority figures, the nature of the relationship has changed. Students are now encouraged to question that authority.

The net effect of the changes in parenting style and availability, and in the educational system, was to create a generation of young people who believed that their preferences and opinions mattered, and were equal in value to the viewpoints of others. Members of older generations, who were raised to respect authority and the opinions of elders, were taken aback when Millennials didn't automatically accept whatever they said.

The Millennial generation entered the workforce at a challenging time. At first, it appeared that the new millennium would get off to a great start, but the enthusiasm that drove up the stock market at the end of the 1990s was exaggerated, and when the bubble popped in late 2000, those expectations were reset. The first decade of the century experienced two recessions, one of which was the worst economic downturn since the Great Depression of the 1930s. Jobs have been scarce since then and wages low, even while employers often ask employees to be on call at any hour, accept jobs without benefits or security, and "recommit" to the company and its mission. As a result, Millennials maintain some distance in their transitional jobs and continue searching for an employer offering better terms.

All Together Now

Traditionalists, Boomers, Xers, and Millennials all had markedly different experiences of life during their formative years. The Silent generation (aka Veterans or Traditionalists) experienced the Great Depression and WWII, times of scarcity and sacrifice that no other generation in the workforce today experienced or can even imagine. They chose not to make waves and were grateful to have work in the 1940s and '50s, and they still are today. Boomers, on the other hand, grew up during a period of unprecedented growth and progress and were encouraged to socialize and to explore themselves. The growth that fueled the optimism came to an abrupt end just as Generation X came on the scene. Left to fend for themselves in one-parent homes after school, Xers graduated into "McJobs." Not wanting a repeat of what had happened to the X Generation, Millennials' parents spent as much spare time with their children as possible.

The next chapter looks at some of the challenges created by having members of these different age-cohort-cultures working together in age-diverse teams.

Endnotes

1. Ernst & Young, LLC. (2013). Younger managers rise in the ranks: EY study on generational shifts in the workplace. http://www.ey.com/US/en/Careers/Fall-2013-Edition-of-EY-Navigator---6---Younger-managers-rise-in-the-ranks.

2. These are sometimes referred to as *maturational theory* and *life course theory*. Strictly speaking, these are not theories. The popular and academic literatures use both "theory" and "perspective." Accordingly, we use both terms.

3. Tulgan, B. (1995). *Managing Generation X: How to Bring Out the Best in Young Talent.* Santa Monica, CA: Merritt Publishing.

4. Tulgan, B. (1995). *Managing Generation X: How to Bring Out the Best in Young Talent.* Santa Monica, CA: Merritt Publishing, p. 18.

5. Zemke, R., Raines, C., & Filipczak, B. (2000). *Generations at Work: Managing the Clash of Veterans, Boomers, Xers, and Nexters in Your Workplace.* New York: AMACOM.

6. Mannheim, K. (1952). *Essays in the Sociology of Knowledge.* London: Routledge and Kegan Paul.

7. Wells Fargo Bank. (2014). 2014 Wells Fargo Millennial study. https://www08.wellsfargomedia.com/downloads/pdf/com/retirement-employee-benefits/insights/2014-millennial-study-summary.pdf.

8. Ehley, B. (2015). "Irresponsible" Millennials saving more than almost every other group. http://www.thefiscaltimes.com/2015/02/25/Irresponsible-Millennials-Saving-More-Almost-Every-Other-Group.

9. Zemke, R., Raines, C., & Filipczak, B. (2000). *Generations at Work: Managing the Clash of Veterans, Boomers, Xers, and Nexters in Your Workplace.* New York: AMACOM.

10. Johnson, M., & Johnson, L. (2010). *Generations, Inc.: From Boomers to Linksters—Managing the Friction Between Generations at Work.* New York: AMACOM.

11. Zemke, R., Raines, C., & Filipczak, B. (2000). *Generations at Work: Managing the Clash of Veterans, Boomers, Xers, and Nexters in Your Workplace.* New York: AMACOM.

12. Strauss, W., & Howe, N. (1991). *Generations: The History of America's Future, 1584 to 2069.* New York: Quill.

13. In *Managing the Millennials* (Espinoza et al., 2010), we refer to this group as the Builder generation. Very few authors currently use the *Builder* label. In this book, we use Silent in deference to the emergent trend in the field.

14. Spock, B. (1946). *Dr. Spock's Baby and Child Care.* New York: Pocket Books.

15. Coupland, D. (1991). *Generation X.* New York: St. Martin's Press.

16. Ramey, G., & Ramey, V. A. (2010). *The rug rat race.* National Bureau of Economic Research. http://www.nber.org/papers/w15284.

7

Dynamics of a Multigenerational Workforce

I n the past 10 years, more than 200 books have been published about the difficulties of managing a multigenerational workforce, and the number of articles in the business and popular media is many times larger. Most of these writings are based on the authors' experiences.

In this chapter, we draw on the growing base of academic research devoted to understanding the work-related values, attitudes, behaviors, and characteristics that lead to intergenerational friction in the workplace. A lot of work has been done over the past few years to develop a better understanding of the causes of this friction. The research shows that there are real differences that distinguish one generation from the next. But more importantly, there are very strong perceptions, some more justified than others, that may lead to friction in your environment. By understanding what underlies these perceptions, and their dynamics, you will be able to inspire your team to function at a higher level.

Managing Generation X[1] was published 20 years ago. Reading it today, it is clear that perceptions of Xers in the workplace have changed over time, even while media stereotypes have stubbornly remained unchanged. But that does not diminish the importance of today's perceptions. Perceptions drive important decisions. Stereotypes are known to influence hiring, promotion, and compensation decisions.[2]

In 2009, the Conference Board of Canada published the results of its study of generational differences in the workplace.[3] The study included Millennials, Gen Xers, and Baby Boomers. The Conference Board administered a two-part questionnaire. The first part consisted of 20 statements, which are listed in Table 7.1 (and repeated in Tables 7.2 and 7.3). Participants in the study were asked simply whether they agreed or disagreed that the statements accurately described their own generation. Next, they were asked whether those same statements were applicable to the two other generations in the study. In the second part, respondents were asked whether 60 additional statements applied to them personally.

The Conference Board study shows that Boomers, Xers, and Millennials all tend to see themselves differently than others see them. There were a few cases in which one generation agreed with how another saw itself, but for the most part, there was relatively little agreement. Respondents' perceptions of their own generation were more favorable than their perceptions of other generations. This was true for respondents from all generations.

The perceptions reported in the study closely parallel generational stereotypes found in the popular media. Millennials were viewed as comfortable with technology and adaptable but somewhat disloyal and difficult to manage. Boomers were generally seen by the other genera-tions as loyal and results-oriented yet not overly adaptable—especially with respect to their comfort with technology. Gen Xers were perceived by the other generations to be skilled in multitasking and willing to learn new things but also somewhat independent and skeptical of author-ity. Out of all of the 60 behavior-by-generation ratings, there was only one in which all three generations agreed: Respondents from all gen-erations were unanimous in viewing Millennials as "comfortable with technology."

We will take a closer look at issues on which the generations agreed and disagreed after reviewing how each generation perceived itself.

Table 7.1 shows how Boomers were rated by themselves, by Xers, and by Millennials. The last column shows the consensus rating, which is the average of the ratings given by members of all three generations. Table 7.2 shows how Gen X was rated, and Table 7.3 shows the ratings for the Millennial generation. These results are based on responses from 304 Boomers, 300 Xers, and 306 Millennials.

Keep in mind that these are perceptions, not objective measurements. However, because we are discussing relationships between groups, perceptions might be more important than any objective measures available.

Table 7.1 Baby Boom Generation: Percentage Agreement by Boomers, Xers, and Millennials

Statement	Self	Xers	Millennials	Average
Open to change	48	27	19	31.3
Skilled in multitasking	74	41	39	51.3
Comfortable with technology	57	33	25	38.3
Willing to learn new things	66	36	35	45.7
Asks for help when needed	62	46	42	50.0
Accepts diversity	63	46	41	50.0
Listens carefully	73	56	49	59.3
Results-driven	79	59	58	65.3
Accepts authority	76	60	51	62.3
Doesn't require close supervision	71	53	48	57.3
Emphasizes following procedures	74	66	63	67.7
Likes to work alone	45	43	48	45.3
Shares information	70	50	52	57.3
Gives maximum effort	81	64	42	62.3
Enjoys working in teams	56	41	30	42.3
Likes informality	45	34	24	34.3
Seeks work-life balance	71	59	55	61.7
Knows how to get what they want	74	63	61	66.0
Trusts the organization	50	54	54	52.7

Statement	Self	Xers	Millennials	Average
Plans to remain with the organization	80	73	71	74.7
TOTAL	1,315	1,004	907	1,075.3

Adapted from the Conference Board of Canada (2009) Winning the "Generation Wars": Making the most of generational differences and similarities in the workplace.[4]

Let us first look at how Boomers rated their own generation, before we continue to the next two tables. Boomers see themselves as loyal (plans to remain with the organization = 80%, accepts authority = 76%) and effective (gives maximum effort = 80%, results-driven = 79%, doesn't require close supervision = 71%, emphasizes following procedures = 74%, knows how to get what they want, skilled in multitasking).

Boomers see themselves as not very open to change but willing to learn new things. Boomers also see themselves as not particularly interested in working alone and having a very slight dislike for informality.

Comparing the Self (Boomers self ratings), Xers, and Millennials columns in Table 7.1, it is evident that Baby Boomers perceive their own generation to be higher on each of the 20 characteristics than Gen Xers or Millennials see them.

Everyone agrees that Boomers:

- Trust the organization
- Plan to remain with the organization
- Are ambivalent about working alone

On the other hand, there are some sizable discrepancies between how Boomers rated themselves and how Millennials and Xers rated them. For Boomers, the areas with the biggest disconnects between how Boomers saw themselves and how the other generations viewed them are:

- Willing to learn new things
- Gives maximum effort
- Skilled in multitasking
- Comfortable with technology
- Open to change

Table 7.2 Generation X: Percentage Agreement by Boomers, Xers, and Millennials

Statement	Boomers	Self	Millennials	Average
Open to change	69	79	64	70.7
Skilled in multitasking	67	80	68	71.7
Comfortable with technology	83	87	76	82.0
Willing to learn new things	79	86	72	79.0
Asks for help when needed	52	68	54	58.0
Accepts diversity	70	82	71	74.3
Listens carefully	43	54	51	49.3
Results-driven	53	73	68	64.7
Accepts authority	44	52	51	49.0
Doesn't require close supervision	26	41	42	36.3
Emphasizes following procedures	30	43	37	36.7
Likes to work alone	28	42	30	33.3
Shares information	60	70	62	64.0
Gives maximum effort	45	64	54	54.3
Enjoys working in teams	62	62	58	60.7
Likes informality	72	73	58	67.7
Seeks work-life balance	62	75	65	67.3
Knows how to get what they want	56	61	60	59.0
Trusts the organization	29	32	43	34.7
Plans to remain with the organization	28	37	48	37.7
TOTAL	1,058	1,261	1,132	1,150.3

Adapted from the Conference Board of Canada (2009) Winning the "Generation Wars": Making the most of generational differences and similarities in the workplace.[5]

Table 7.2 tells us that everyone agrees that Generation X is comfortable with technology, is willing to learn new things, accepts diversity, is skilled in multitasking, is open to change, enjoys working in teams, does not like working alone, and does not trust the organization or plan to stay long.

There are a few discrepancies, however. Xers saw themselves as significantly higher in giving maximum effort than either Boomers or

Millennials saw them. Also, Millennials rated Xers much lower on liking informality and much higher on trusting the organization. Similarly, Boomers are ambivalent about Xers being results-driven, while Xers rated themselves fairly highly.

Table 7.3   Millennials: Percentage Agreement by Boomers, Xers, and Millennials

Statement	Boomers	Xers	Self	Average
Open to change	64	70	81	71.7
Skilled in multitasking	43	50	68	53.7
Comfortable with technology	84	84	84	84.0
Willing to learn new things	70	72	81	74.3
Asks for help when needed	37	48	62	49.0
Accepts diversity	68	75	83	75.3
Listens carefully	16	24	42	27.3
Results-driven	29	33	53	38.3
Accepts authority	20	24	46	30.0
Doesn't require close supervision	6	8	17	10.3
Emphasizes following procedures	11	17	27	18.3
Likes to work alone	24	26	35	28.3
Shares information	41	51	66	52.7
Gives maximum effort	20	24	42	28.7
Enjoys working in teams	50	63	67	60.0
Likes informality	70	75	77	74.0
Seeks work-life balance	44	46	59	49.7
Knows how to get what they want	30	30	42	34.0
Trusts the organization	11	22	31	21.3
Plans to remain with the organization	7	10	24	13.7
TOTAL	745	852	1,087	894.7

·Adapted from the Conference Board of Canada (2009) Winning the "Generation Wars": Making the most of generational differences and similarities in the workplace.[6]

Everyone agrees that Millennials:

- Are comfortable with technology
- Are willing to learn new things

- Like informality
- Require supervision
- Plan to leave
- Don't follow procedures
- Don't like to work alone
- Accept diversity

The areas with the biggest disconnect between how Millennials perceived themselves and how the other generations saw them are the following:

- Listens carefully
- Results-driven
- Accepts authority
- Gives maximum effort
- Asks for help when needed
- Shares information

Again, we hasten to point out that these are *perceptions*. However, they are also challenges to be addressed.

Here are some things that jump out at us when we compare all three tables:

- No one is particularly good at listening. Boomers rate their generational cohort fairly high on this behavior (73% of Boomers agree that Boomers listen carefully), but Millennials and Xers disagree sharply. The average rating for all groups by all groups is below 50%.
- Sharing information seems to be a challenge for everyone.
- Boomers rated themselves higher overall (1,315) than Xers rated themselves (1,261) or Millennials (1,087).

- Xers had the highest average rating (1,150) compared to Boomers (1,075) and Millennials (894).

- Millennials and Boomers have the biggest disconnect. They are the farthest apart in how they see each other.

As a whole, each generation saw itself more favorably than the others saw it. This is consistent with the tendency for people to rate themselves favorably. This tendency is well known among social scientists. Cognitive psychologists have documented a number of perceptual biases related to this tendency.

For a few attributes, the discrepancy in perceptions is quite large. For example, Baby Boomers saw themselves as far more open to change, skilled in multitasking, comfortable with technology, willing to learn new things, sharing of information, giving of effort, and team oriented than Xers or Millennials saw them. Likewise, Millennials saw themselves as far more skilled in multitasking, asking for help, careful listeners, accepting of authority, and sharing of information than Boomers or Xers saw them.

In contrast, there is relatively little disagreement about Generation X.

We provide a brief overview of perceptual biases and then examine several of the larger perceptual gaps in detail below.

Perceptual Biases

Attribution theory is a model of how people attribute responsibility for an event. Attribution theory describes two biases that are really two sides of the same coin. The first bias, called the *fundamental attribution error*, is the tendency to attribute poor outcomes in others to some internal flaw in the other's character. The corollary to the fundamental attribution error is the self-serving bias, in which individuals tend to excuse themselves for their own lapses. The self-serving bias, for example, leads us to continue to see ourselves as punctual even as we arrive late to a meeting because, after all, it's not our fault if the barista got our drink order wrong three times in a row.

Another example is the overconfidence bias. This is a more general tendency to overrate our ability or contribution. The most humorous demonstration of this comes from couples who are each asked to estimate their contribution to the household chores. Each member is asked privately to estimate his or her individual contribution. When the totals are added up, it seems that each couple is benefitting from a combined 140% contribution!

Identifying Biases in the Conference Board Results

There appear to be many examples of perceptual biases at work in the Canadian Conference Board data. For example, the first line of Table 7.1 shows that 48% of Baby Boomers who participated in this study agreed that Boomers are open to change. However, just 27% of Gen Xers agreed, and only 19% of Millennials agreed that Boomers are open to change.

As you can see, there is a pretty wide gap in perceptions. Thirty-one percent of all of the survey respondents together on average agreed that Boomers are open to change. Gen Xers were just slightly below the multi-generational average, meaning they are most accurate in their perceptions. Boomers' perception of themselves is 17% above the average, indicating they have a significantly inflated view of their own openness to change, while Millennials' perception of Boomers is 12% below the average.

The gaps are even larger for the next item, skilled in multitasking. Forty-one percent of Xers and 39% of Millennials agreed that Boomers are skilled in multitasking, whereas 74% of Boomers thought the statement was accurate. This could be the result of a difference in interpretation of what multitasking means between the different cohorts. It might be that for Boomers, multitasking means managing more than one project at a time or working down a list of tasks that need to be accomplished during the day, whereas for Millennials, multitasking might mean having multiple chat sessions open on their desktop while working on a spreadsheet and listening to a podcast. We don't have the answer. A perceptual gap of this magnitude indicates that the concept of multitasking is not the same for the three groups.

The Conference Board of Canada report does not address whether the study participants all interpreted the survey questions the same way. However, another team of researchers did address this problem. John Meriac and Christina Banister of the University of Missouri and David Woehr of the University of Tennessee conducted a study using a survey instrument called the Multidimensional Work Ethic Profile (MWEP), in which they showed that Millennials, Xers, and Boomers interpreted many of the MWEP questions differently.[7] For example, one of the items from the MWEP that is interpreted differently by Boomers and Xers is "By working hard, a person can overcome every obstacle that life presents." Considering what we covered in the last chapter regarding the experiences of Xers growing up, it's easy to see how they might agree that hard work would help to overcome *many* obstacles but not *every* obstacle.

Clearly, Millennials and Xers didn't see Boomers as being nearly as open to change or skilled in multitasking as Boomers saw themselves. Very likely this was the result of the same mental process that causes people to see themselves more favorably than is warranted. However, it doesn't necessarily mean that the observers' (in this case, Gen Xers' and Millennials') views were correct, either. We don't have enough data here to tell what the "real" answer is, but most likely it's somewhere between the three.

Something Else Going on Besides Just Overconfidence

In terms of whether Boomers are skilled in multitasking, Gen Xers agreed 41% and Millennials agreed 39%. Statistically, this is not a significant difference and we can say that Gen Xers and Millennials were in full agreement with one another that Boomers are not particularly good at multitasking. Because there is no meaningful difference between the Millennial and Xer assessments, it seems fair to conclude that there is no Xer or Millennial bias and that their view is closer to the truth.

However, when it comes to openness to change, it seems there might be some additional dynamics that account for the difference in how Xers and Millennials rated Boomers. It might be that Boomers shut down Millennial suggestions substantially more than they do suggestions from Xers. This would cause Millennials to legitimately feel that Boomers are not open to change and to rate Boomers 8% lower than Xers rate them (19% and 27%, respectively).

Something similar might underlie the difference in Millennials' and Xers' perceptions of whether Boomers like informality. Forty-five percent of Boomer respondents agreed that Boomers like informality (Table 7.1, line 16). As with openness to change, Millennials and Xers disagreed with Boomers and each other. Twenty-four percent of Millennials and 34% of Xers agreed that Boomers like informality. Without additional data, we can't know for certain, but it seems probable that something in the Millennials' experience of Boomers accounts for the 10-percentage-point difference. It's easy to imagine that Boomers dislike Millennials' casualness and are not shy about their dislike. Boomers have consistently complained about the Millennials' abrasiveness, and in the same study, Boomers agreed 77% that Millennials like informality. It seems fair to suppose that there might be a little mutual resentment around this issue.

In addition to questions about Boomers, Xers, and Millennials, the Canadian Conference Board also asked respondents to rate themselves on 59 different workplace behaviors in 12 different categories, including teamwork, conscientiousness, sociability, communication style, and intrinsic and extrinsic motivation. Interestingly, for the most part, there is not much difference between the generations. For instance, Boomers, Xers, and Millennials agreed with the statement "I am passionate" 77%, 75%, and 74%, respectively. Boomers, Xers, and Millennials also had very similar levels of agreement with "I like to work in teams" (55%, 57%, and 61%, respectively). This is worth taking a moment to consider. When answering the same question, but with reference to their generation rather than themselves personally, 62% of Xers agreed that Gen Xers enjoy working in teams. For Millennials, the difference when answering on behalf of their generation as opposed to personally was even greater, at 67% versus 61%. Boomers came closest, at 56% (my generation) versus 55% (me). Millennials and Xers showed a little bias in favor of their groups over themselves individually.

However, while Boomers came closest when rating themselves personally versus rating their generation as a whole on being team players, they had the greatest mismatch between how they saw themselves in comparison to how the other generations saw them. Only 30% of Millennials and 41% of Xers agreed that Boomers enjoy working in teams. As with openness to change, we have to assume that some intergenerational dynamic is responsible for this gap. As before, we have to speculate. It's worth noting, before we say anything else, that Boomers rated Xers relatively high here. In fact, Boomers rated Xers higher than they rated themselves. It's also worth noting that Boomers rated Millennials fairly well—not as high as they rated themselves but much higher than Millennials rated Boomers. Finally, Xers give Millennials the highest intergenerational rating. These last three observations suggest that there is no strong bias against Millennials or Xers in this area. Very likely, there is something unintended or unconscious in the behavior of Boomers that Xers and Millennials perceive as exclusionary. It may be that Boomers have greater tenure within their respective organizations and don't extend the same level of effort to interact with others outside their cohort or with "kids" they expect not to stay with the organization for more than 12 months.

This interpretation of the Conference Board of Canada results is consistent with findings from other studies. For example, Scott Lester and colleagues conducted a study in which they asked workers to indicate their preferences for a number of workplace elements, including electronic communications, working in teams, and flexibility. Their key finding was that perceived differences outnumber actual differences.[8] They show that actual preferences are consistent with generational stereotypes but not nearly as great as the stereotypes would lead one to believe.

Communicate, Communicate, Communicate!

Among the biggest challenges in a multigenerational workforce are perceptions that impede communication and positive interaction. As we saw previously, none of the generations were impressed with the others' ability to listen carefully. Also, each cohort rated the others fairly low in asking for help when needed. Millennials and Boomers both rated one another much lower on this behavior than they rated themselves. Very likely, when survey participants answered these questions, they did not think to themselves that "there is another group I could be getting help from—members of another generation that I don't normally interact with." Similarly, Millennials might not observe Boomers asking other Boomers for technical help, and Boomers might not witness Millennials asking each other for help in understanding organizational procedure. The lesson here is that workers need to be made more comfortable initiating informal communication across generational boundaries.

Most of us tend to think we're doing a better job than we in fact are. We tend to overlook evidence that does not support our perceptions. And we tend not to realize when our understanding of a situation is different from how others see it. This is especially difficult when those different understandings are based on different values and different assumptions about how the world works.

We see an opportunity to create a much more fulfilling environment by bridging these communication gaps. Empowered with this understanding and given the characteristics of Millennial managers summarized from our survey in the next chapter, we believe you will be an outstanding leader.

Endnotes

1. Tulgan, B. (1995). *Managing Generation X: How to Bring Out the Best in Young Talent.* Santa Monica, CA: Merritt Publishing.

2. Perry, E. L., Hanvongse, P., & Casoinic, D. A. (2013). Making a case for the existence of generational stereotypes: A literature review and exploratory study. In Field, J., Burke, R. J., & Cooper, C. L. (Eds.), *The SAGE handbook of aging, work and society.* London: Sage.

3. Conference Board of Canada. (2009). Winning the "Generation Wars": Making the most of generational differences and similarities in the workplace. https://www.aqesss.qc.ca/docs/pdf/i-media/20091126/ConferenceBoard_Compete_Generation_Wars.pdf.

4. Conference Board of Canada. (2009). Winning the "Generation Wars": Making the most of generational differences and similarities in the workplace. https://www.aqesss.qc.ca/docs/pdf/i-media/20091126/ConferenceBoard_Compete_Generation_Wars.pdf.

5. Conference Board of Canada. (2009). Winning the "Generation Wars": Making the most of generational differences and similarities in the workplace. https://www.aqesss.qc.ca/docs/pdf/i-media/20091126/ConferenceBoard_Compete_Generation_Wars.pdf.

6. Conference Board of Canada. (2009). Winning the "Generation Wars": Making the most of generational differences and similarities in the workplace. https://www.aqesss.qc.ca/docs/pdf/i-media/20091126/ConferenceBoard_Compete_Generation_Wars.pdf.

7. Meriac, J. P., Woehr, D. J., & Banister, C. (2010). Generational differences in work ethic: An examination of measurement equivalence across three cohorts. *Journal of Business Psychology, 25,* 315–324.

8. Lester, S. W., et al. (2012) Actual versus perceived differences at work: An empirical examination. *Journal of Leadership & Organizational Studies, 19*(3), 341–354.

8

The Reasons You Will Be a Great Leader

"You're probably tired of hearing all of the different labels that others have put on your generation. I'm going to risk one more: the Ben Franklin generation. 'An America led by the Ben Franklin generation is likely to be a more stable, patient, values-driven, and realistic place than the one led by the boomers. It's a place where technology is expected to solve problems, simplify life, and strip inauthenticity out of the sales process. They don't want to beat the system; the success of Wealthfront and others says that the Ben Franklins want a fair system they can be part of, and that can benefit everyone in it.'"

—Adam Hanft, *The Stunning Evolution of Millennials*

We think Millennials are poised to become the greatest generation of managerial leaders seen thus far. That doesn't mean you Millennials won't be eclipsed by yet another generation, but for now you're it...almost. In response to the news that Richard Branson's Virgin Group would begin offering up to 12 months of paternity leave, our friend, an outspoken Millennial leader and manager, posted on Facebook, "I can't wait until the idea of trusting your employees and fostering an environment that breeds happiness in employees is not newsworthy. We have a long way to go but I am inspired by the progress." We expect to see a lot more of this in the future, and the main reason for the change will be the increasing number of Millennials in leadership roles.

In a survey we conducted, we found evidence that Millennial managers are already among the best out there. There are many different ways that managerial quality can be measured. We created our own simple measure, based on Google's Project Oxygen. Then we asked employees to rate their managers using our survey. When we summarized the responses by the age of the survey respondents' managers, we found some surprises you will be very interested in. Table 8.1 summarizes our findings.

Millennial Manager Survey

In 2001, when the company was still young, Google's co-founder Larry Page attempted to eliminate managers entirely. The experiment didn't last long. Later, at the end of the decade, after the company had done nothing but grow, Google set out to find out, in its own way, what makes a good manager. As you would expect from an organization that provides some of the world's best data-driven solutions, the company's People Analytics team crunched project metrics, 360-degree performance reviews, and even exit interviews to find out what makes a good manager.[1]

Google might be the ideal organization in which to conduct a study to find the real value of managers, if any exists, and to determine exactly where that value comes from. Google's culture is dominated by highly motivated engineers. By nature, they are skeptical of managers. They see managers as distracting from the real work of solving problems rather than contributing. Against this background of skepticism, the People Analytics research was able to show which factors in managerial behavior contributed to the organization.

Google has relatively low turnover, and even low-scoring managers are doing pretty well. However, by analyzing the data, the People Analytics team was able to show that a strong relationship existed between managerial quality, satisfaction, and turnover. The analysis revealed that employees with high-scoring managers "consistently reported greater satisfaction in a number of areas including innovation, work-life balance, and career development."[2]

Continuing the research, the People Analytics team next conducted a series of double-blind qualitative interviews to learn what exactly led to a manager being "high scoring." The analysis revealed the following list of behaviors that differentiated "high quality" from "low quality" managers, in order according to their importance:

- Good coach

- Empowers the team

- Expresses interest in, and concern for, team members' success and well-being

- Is productive and results oriented

- Is a good communicator—listens and shares information

- Helps with career development

- Has a clear vision and strategy for the team

- Has key technical skills that help him or her advise the team[3]

Our survey was designed in part around Google's eight managerial behaviors. The literature on Millennials describes them as having been socialized to work with partners and in teams to a greater extent than previous generations. A recent survey by MSLGroup found that Millennials see coaching as an important part of the supervisor-employee relationship, and they eschew the hierarchical, power-oriented management role that is more typical of older generations. As employees, Millennials seek high levels of support from their managers.[4] Assuming that they treat others in the way that they would like to be treated, we expect Millennials to manage with a low power orientation—that is, a more inclusive and transparent style of delegation and oversight in which authority is de-emphasized and constructive feedback is expected. We hypothesized that Millennials would rank higher than others in terms of the more team-related behaviors. At the same time, we hypothesized that they would be below the mean in areas requiring more experience.

Table 8.1 shows the percentage of respondents who answered either "Strongly Agree" or "Agree" to each behavior when considering their own manager. The percentages are summarized by the age of the survey participants' direct supervisors. (Participants estimated the ages of their supervisors.)

The survey was conducted in 2015, so anyone in the survey 34 years old and under was a Millennial at that time.

Table 8.1 Percentage of Respondents Who Strongly Agreed or Agreed About Their Own Manager, By Age of Manager

| Question | Manager's Age | | | | | | |
	18–24	25–34	35–44	45–54	55–64	65+	Avg.
Does your manager communicate clearly with your team?	69	67	67	59	60	56	65
Your manager cares about team members' success and well-being.	77	77	63	70	58	78	71
Your manager helps subordinates with career development.	54	59	56	61	45	67	57
Your manager empowers his/her employees.	54	73	63	64	48	56	66
Would you say your manager is a good coach?	62	72	69	64	58	78	68

	Manager's Age						
Question	18–24	25–34	35–44	45–54	55–64	65+	Avg.
Your manager listens to what you have to say.	62	72	69	59	63	78	68
Would you say that your manager is results oriented?	85	74	60	83	73	67	73
Your manager has the technical skills required for the job.	78	78	78	78	53	100	75
Your manager has a clear vision for the team.	67	69	65	69	53	83	67

The results for Millennial managers exceeded our expectations. We anticipated that they would do well, but we were actually quite impressed. The 25- to 34-year-olds were ahead of all other age groups in empowering their employees. Overall, 25- to 34-year-olds came out either first or second on all but two of the nine dimensions. The only group with a higher overall rating was the managers 65 years and up, which is remarkable considering that Millennial managers have considerably less experience than managers from other cohorts.

It is natural to wonder if this assessment is actually a consequence of inexperience. Perhaps it's just that Millennial managers are still fresh and have not been in the work world long enough to have been worn down by stress and long hours on challenging projects. But we don't think so. We expect that managers who excel in these areas will continue to perform better and to be positively reinforced in a self-reinforcing cycle.

We did not expect to see the managers over age 65 rated so highly by their employees. They received the highest ratings on six of the nine behaviors. They really stand out from the crowd in having a clear vision for the team and possessing the required technical skills. They also showed a strong lead in being good coaches and listening to what employees have to say.

The age 65 and older managers assessed in our survey are most likely at a point in their careers where they are no longer trying to advance. They have the skills they need to do their jobs (100% agreement) and have chosen not to retire. Most likely they enjoy what they do. They know what they're doing (83% agreement), and they care about the people they work with (78% agreement). Because they like what they do, care about their employees, and are satisfied with where they are in their careers, they are less focused on the results and more focused on the people. Because they are where they want to be, doing what they want to be doing, these managers are better listeners, better coaches, and better at helping subordinates with career development.

Millennial managers were ranked much higher overall on the ratings than one might expect, although there's a clear distinction between the 18–24 and 25–34 age groups. The older Millennial group was very close behind the 65+ managers on key managerial behaviors.

In terms of empowering their employees, 25- to 34-year-old managers are the clear leaders. Consistent with Millennial values, they demonstrate care for their employees. Although trailing the 65+ managers, they still excel in listening and coaching. We expect improvement over time as they gain experience. We expect to see even larger improvements in communicating with the team, expressing a vision, and helping subordinates with career development.

In contrast to the older Millennial group, 18- to 24-year-old managers are the clear leaders in terms of being results oriented. Otherwise, they trail behind the elder Millennials but are still ahead of everyone else except the 65+ group. It is easy to think that those individuals in the 18–24 group who are bringing up the average on the "results oriented" dimension are not cut from the same cloth as the older Millennials, that perhaps they are simply go-getters who advanced by pushing their employees. But look closely at the differences between the two Millennial age groups. They have nearly identical scores in four of the categories, which indicates that the two groups are actually very similar. The younger managers are weakest in terms of empowering their employees and helping with career development. It is worth noting that none of the groups are very good on this dimension. The overall average is 57%. But for empowering employees, the difference is substantial. It appears that 18- to 24-year-old managers may have attained their leadership roles by focusing on results that they were able to achieve despite their lack of experience by directing rather than empowering their employees. It is therefore significant that they were still recognized as caring about their employees at the same level (77%) as the 25- to 34-year-olds.

Not to sound too gushy or anything, but we think you Millennials are riding a wave. There has been a long-term trend toward more human-centered organizations. We see a number of trends heading in the right direction, and the incoming crop of young managers are bringing with them the values, attitudes, and tools to see these changes through.

In his book *The Human Equation*, Jeffrey Pfeffer explains that businesses succeed on the basis of how they treat and manage their people more than anything else.[5] One of the companies Pfeffer studied was Southwest Airlines, which boasts some impressive statistics. Southwest has been profitable in all but two of the past 40 years. (During the same period, many competing airlines declared bankruptcy or went out of business entirely.) If you had purchased $1,000 worth of LUV stock in 1980, you could have sold it for more than $200,000 at the beginning of 2015. The same investment made in an S&P 500 mutual fund would have grown to $17,400. Very few companies achieve such staggering outperformance.

How does a company like Southwest Airlines achieve growth of around 18%, sustained over several decades? Herb Kelleher, founder of Southwest, explains his company's success like this:

> The business of business is people, yesterday, today, and forever. Among employees, shareholders, and customers, we decided that our internal customers, our employees, came first. The synergy in our opinion is simple—honor, respect, care for, protect, and reward your employees regardless of title or position, and in turn they will treat each other and your external customers in a warm, caring, and hospitable way. This causes external customers to return, thus bringing joy to shareholders. We believe that our job is to not only provide a far more reliable service, at far lower fares, but also to provide a spiritual infusion, an infusion of fun, warmth, hospitality, and diligent servanthood for both employees and our passengers. The intangibles of spirit in our view, are more important than the tangibles of things. Why? First of all, it's a matter of morality and ethics. But secondly, from a purely business standpoint, the tangibles can always be purchased. All airlines have airplanes. But the intangibles are far more difficult for competitors to replicate....Show that you value your employees as individuals, not just as workers, through word and deed.[6]

Rather than being a fluke, Pfeffer found that Southwest is representative of a small number of organizations that defy the conventional wisdom that employees are simply an expense to be squeezed when times are tough. Although the trend toward downsizing has accelerated in the post-Great Recession economy, it is not possible that such a strong source of competitive advantage will be ignored indefinitely. Richard Branson has gotten the message. Tony Hsieh, CEO of Zappos, has gotten the message.

In its third annual Millennial Survey (which included 7,800 partici-pants from 28 countries), Deloitte found that most see business hav-ing positive impact on society but think business can do much more.[7] Fifty percent of the respondents want to work for an ethical business. The majority of the respondents said they prefer organizations with open, transparent, and inclusive leadership styles. You are coming of age at a time when the value of people in an organization is beginning to be understood and appreciated. Although such a perspective has not yet been adopted everywhere, organizations that embrace the mind-set have been well studied. Values espoused by Millennials are consistent with the findings of researchers who have studied these organizations.

Deloitte compared the management priorities of Millennials and Baby Boomers. Deloitte asked Gen Y respondents to compare their own pri-orities to what they perceive the priorities to be for senior leaders in their organizations. Millennials emphasized employee well-being at a significantly higher rate (37% versus 17%) than their corporate leaders. They also valued employee growth and development (32% versus 18%) and making positive contributions to local communities/society (27% versus 18%) at much higher rates. These values are consistent with the style of management espoused by Herb Kelleher and other leaders who put employees first, and with the behaviors that we found in our own survey.

Millennials display surprising strength in key areas of managerial com-petency, especially given their relative youth. The competencies were originally identified using rigorous analysis in an organization skeptical of the concept of management. It is important to recognize that these strengths are consistent with the principles of "people centered" man-agement, an approach that has been shown to be associated with higher levels of employee engagement and satisfaction, as well as spectacular organizational growth. Managerial leaders who excel in these compe-tences will be leading the pack very shortly.

The next chapter focuses on what makes Millennials tick in the workplace and how you can leverage your strengths as a manager to bring out the best in them.

Endnotes

1. Garvin, D. A. (2013). How Google sold its engineers on management. *Harvard Business Review, 91*(12), 74–82.

2. Garvin, D. A. (2013). How Google sold its engineers on management. *Harvard Business Review, 91*(12), 77.

3. Garvin, D. A. (2013). How Google sold its engineers on management. *Harvard Business Review, 91*(12), 78.

4. MSLGroup. (2014). Millennial compass report: The Millennial generation in the workplace. http://www.scribd.com/doc/211602632/The-Millennial-Compass-The-Millennial-Generation-In-The-Workplace.

5. Pfeffer, J. (1998). *The Human Equation: Building Profits by Putting People First.* Cambridge, MA: Harvard Business School Press.

6. Kelleher, H. (2008). Building a people-focused culture. Paper presented at World of Business Ideas (previously HSM). https://www.youtube.com/watch?v=oxTFA1kh1m8.

7. Deloitte (2015). Mind the gaps: The 2015 Deloitte Millennial Survey. www.deloitte.com/MillennialSurvey.

9

Managing Millennials

"Love is the killer app. Those of us who use love as a point of differen-
tiation in business will separate ourselves from our competitors just as
world-class distance runners separate themselves from the rest of the
pack trailing behind them."

—Tim Sanders, *Love Is the Killer App*

I n this chapter, we address how you can help Millennials get what they want out of work and overcome challenges they face. There is no doubt you will still identify with many of the frustrations Millennials report experiencing at work—and that should give you additional insight and be incredibly helpful on many levels, particularly when it comes to empathy, understanding, and giving helpful advice.

Some Advice About Giving Advice

One note of caution about giving advice: Be sure to begin with the expe-rience of your employee and not your own. Ask first about her experi-ence. That is also a good idea when managing people older than you, but you will see in the following list of challenges that lack of experience is the number-one roadblock Millennials report facing. They are often in a position of having less experience than others. Experience is repeat-edly offered as the reason they don't get hired, promoted, listened to, or respected. When something is thrown at you over and over, a natural reaction is to be dismissive of it. As one young worker said, "Experience is overrated!" You don't have to agree with the statement, but you can certainly understand the frustration behind it.

It could be argued that in 2008, Millennials put President Obama into the Whitehouse because they related to his inexperience. His two major competitors ran on the platform of having decades of experience. Not possessing nearly as much experience as his political foes (Clinton and McCain), Obama ran on a platform of having good judgment. The message resonated with Millennials. If your employees do not have a whole lot of experience, try engaging them with what they think.

Work Is Culture Shock

It became very clear to us early in our work that Millennials experience culture shock when they transition from college life to work. While in school, they eagerly anticipate making the transition into a career, but when they finally get there, it is not entirely what they expected. As an example, our research participants talked about the pressure and responsibility of transitioning to professional life from a college lifestyle they were familiar with and enjoyed. One interviewee lamented, "It has been a challenge to adjust from a laissez-faire work structure in college to the highly regimented culture of a large corporation."

Based on challenges Millennials report facing, it is obvious that *work* isn't all they thought it would be. The greatest and yet most basic expectation Millennials have is for the authority figures in their lives to be supporting, affirming, and committed to their success. For many, work is the first environment they encounter in which they do not feel supported or affirmed or that someone cares about their success. While other generations may have also experienced a form of culture shock upon entering the workforce, we argue that it is more acute with Millennials because they have grown up in a world committed to their success.

Your perspective can make all the difference in the world with respect to how effectively Millennials make the transition. One manager (not a Millennial) we interviewed emphatically told us, "They are here to make me look good, not the other way around." You can share such a perspective, but you will have to accept the consequences—absenteeism, low commitment, and high turnover. It is well documented that people quit managers, not companies. We are not suggesting that you subjugate the success of the company, roll out the red carpet, and become a personal butler. Millennials are natural collaborators and problem-solvers because they are always searching for a third way to look at things. It does not have to be "You are here to make me look good" or "I am here to make you look good." You really can have it a third way. The reality is, there is nothing wrong with investing in the success of your Millennials or making them look good. In the end, it will make you look great.

Managers Who Get It and Managers Who Don't

Let's begin with our early efforts at trying to understand generational tension in the workplace. If you recall, our intrigue about Millennials was inspired in the classroom. As is the case with all engaging research projects, curiosity is the precursor to inquiry. We wanted to move beyond our experience to see how managers were experiencing Millennials in the workplace.

The research design called upon human resource directors to identify six people in their respective companies for the study. Each company was requested to provide three managers effective at managing Millennials and three considered to be challenged. We conducted one-on-one interviews followed by a focus group with all six participants. We did the focus groups because we wanted to observe the dynamic between the effective and challenged managers. We were especially curious to see if the effective and challenged managers would contradict one another in a semi-public setting.

There was virtually no disagreement among the managers. Both groups perceived Millennials as entitled and abrasive. However, that is where the similarity ended. Table 9.1 presents a list of key differences the study found between the two groups of managers.

Table 9.1 Effective Managers Versus Challenged Managers[1]

Perspective	Effective Managers	Challenged Managers
Adaptability	Talked about their own need to change in order to manage in "today's world."	Talked about how others needed to change to make it in the "real world."
Self-efficacy	Believed there was something they could do about the situation.	Believed that there was very little they could do about the situation.
Confidence	Allowed their subordinates to challenge them (ideas, processes, ways of doing things).	Sanctioned or punished their subordinates for challenging them.
Power	Used the power of relationship versus the power of their position.	Felt the only power they had was their positional authority.
Energy	Working with Millennials made them feel younger.	Working with Millennials made them feel older.
Success	Saw themselves as key to the Millennials' success.	Saw the Millennials as an impediment to their own success.

Upon displaying the comparison of the effective versus challenged managers, we are often asked the question "Isn't that just good management?" Our answer is "Yes. However, it happens to be exponentially important when managing Millennials." It is particularly critical when it comes to your perspective on success. Millennials need to know that you care about their development, have a plan, and are willing to sponsor them. It is a bottom-line expectation.

Next we will share how managers perceive Millennials in the workplace. These are the perceptions that both challenged and effective managers agreed on in our focus groups.

Manager Perceptions of Millennials

It has been said that perception (the way you think about or understand someone or something) is not necessarily reality—but perception can create reality. We vetted manager perceptions with Millennials because we were concerned that the terms would be considered too pejorative. To our surprise and relief, the Millennial focus groups recommended that we keep the terms.

Table 9.2 compares manager perceptions of Millennials with Millennials' intrinsic values. As you can see, the values are very positive; however, they are often manifested in behaviors that get misinterpreted by managers:

Table 9.2 Manager Perceptions Compared with Millennial Intrinsic Values[2]

Millennials Intrinsic Value	Manager Perception	Description of Perception
Work-life fusion	Autonomous	Millennials express a desire to do what they want when they want, have the schedule they want, and not worry about someone micromanaging them. They don't feel they should have to conform to office processes as long as they complete their work.
Reward	Entitled	Millennials express that they deserve to be recognized and rewarded. They want to move up the ladder quickly but not always on managements' terms. They want a guarantee for their performance, not just the opportunity to perform.
Self-expression	Imaginative	Millennials are recognized for having a great "imagination" and can offer a fresh perspective and unique insight into a myriad of situations. Their imagination can distract them from participating in an ordered or mechanistic process or from focusing on solutions that are viable under organizational constraints like timelines and budgets.

Millennials Intrinsic Value	Manager Perception	Description of Perception
Attention	Self-absorbed	Millennials are perceived to be primarily concerned with how they are treated rather than how they treat others. Tasks are seen as a means to their ends. Millennials are often preoccupied with their own personal need for trust, encouragement, and praise.
Achievement	Defensive	Millennials often experience anger, guardedness, offense, and resentment, and they shift responsibility in response to critique and evaluation. They want to be told when they are doing well but not when they are doing poorly.
Informality	Abrasive	Perhaps due to technology, Millennial communication style can be experienced as curt. They are perceived to be inattentive to social courtesies like knowing when to say thank you and please. Whether intentional or not, their behavior is interpreted as disrespectful or usurping authority.
Simplicity	Myopic	Millennials struggle with cause-and-effect relationships. The struggle is perceived as a narrow-sightedness guided by internal interests, without an understanding of how others and the organization are impacted.
Multitasking	Unfocused	Millennials, as a cohort, are recognized for their intellectual ability but are often perceived to struggle with a lack of attention to detail. They have a hard time staying focused on tasks for which they have no interest.
Meaning	Indifferent	Millennials are perceived as careless, apathetic, or lacking commitment.

Rather than get frustrated and complain about what Millennials are like, effective managers practice the competencies listed in Table 9.3. It is important to note that Millennials who manage express similar perceptions of Millennials and tend to be more critical of their peers.

To reiterate, the following competencies are good management in general but are exponentially important when managing people your age or younger. In Table 9.3, we match managerial competencies to perceived orientations and intrinsic values possessed by Millennials.

Table 9.3 Perceived Orientations, Millennials' Intrinsic Values, and Required Managerial Competencies[3]

Perceived Orientation	Millennial Intrinsic Value	Required Managerial Competency
Autonomous	Work-life fusion	Be flexible
Entitled	Reward	Create the right rewards
Imaginative	Self-expression	Put their imagination to work
Self-absorbed	Attention	Build a relationship
Defensive	Achievement	Be positive when correcting
Abrasive	Informality	Don't take things personally
Myopic	Simplicity	Show the big picture
Unfocused	Multitasking	Include the details
Indifferent	Meaning	Make it matter to them

Managerial Leader Competencies Needed for Managing Millennials

We discovered nine managerial competencies essential to managing Millennials. The competencies are not only useful in reducing tension between managers and Millennials—they help to create an environment in which both can thrive.

Be Flexible

Focus more on what gets done than on how it gets done and give Millennials the leeway to work how they want when possible. When possible, give Millennials the freedom to accomplish work in their own way.

Create the Right Rewards

Acknowledge the contribution of Millennials. Managers can reward desired behavior with something as simple as verbal recognition. For larger successes, focus on bigger rewards, like a promotion, bonus, or more opportunities. Rewards don't need to be overdone for every accomplishment, but Millennials should be recognized when things go well.

Put Their Imagination to Work

Keep Millennials' minds (and hearts) engaged by using their well-developed imagination to solve problems and innovate. Millennials grew up learning to develop and use creativity. As a result, they are full of ideas they are eager to share. By giving them opportunities to use their creativity, organizations can benefit from Millennials' imagination and energy.

Build a Relationship

This should be the easiest skill for a Millennial manager. Instead of treating Millennial employees as subordinates and expecting them to do what they are told (when they are told), connect relationally with them first. Many Millennials have been taught throughout their lives to focus first on their own needs and success. Managers who show interest and create personal connections with them will earn trust and have better working relationships.

Be Positive When Correcting

Avoid defensive reactions to direct criticism by reducing conflict, disarming Millennial employees, and focusing on areas of improvement as a positive. Prior to entering the workplace, many Millennials received praise simply for participating in activities. If correction was needed, it was softened to make it easier to hear. Often, this leads to defensiveness when faced with criticism that is not so soft. Managers can reduce conflict by taking extra time to focus on timely, frequent, and constructive feedback.

Don't Take Things Personally

As discussed in Chapter 4, "Be True to You," adapt to Millennials' brief, frank communication style and don't take offense. Keep the focus on them and their development. They are sure to challenge your authority in every way you can imagine. You have to self-differentiate and understand what they are doing and why they are doing it—and not react.

Show the Big Picture

Explain to Millennials the reasons for doing their work, why it matters, and what depends on them doing a good job. Share your expertise. Millennials can appear narrow-sighted due to a lack of experience or having worked in overstructured workplaces. It may be harder for them to see the big picture. Show them how other employees, departments, and downstream processes consume their output, and how those jobs depend on the quality of your employee's work. Successful managers can help Millennials make the connection between everyday tasks and overall results.

Include the Details

Help your Millennial employees overcome the numerous distractions and "multitasking overload" with details they need about the work they are doing and the results you are expecting. Millennials can be very motivated and focused on tasks that interest them but may be easily distracted from tasks that don't. When managers give specific details and explain the results they expect, Millennial employees are better at staying focused. Managers need to communicate clear information without assuming that they've been understood.

Make It Matter to Them

Understand what Millennials care about and help them tie what they are working on to something meaningful for them. Millennials care deeply about the things that interest them, but they can also seem uncaring about others' concerns if they don't understand the reasons for them. Successful managers connect their employees' aspirations to organizational objectives.

Okay, we have opened a treasure chest of information. It is now time to get into how Millennials experience the workplace.

The Biggest Challenges Millennials Report Facing in the Workplace

Ron Weber, a workforce development guru, read the book *Managing the Millennials* and asked Chip to keynote at a corporate event in Chicago. When asked who the audience would be, Ron said they were all college new hires. After seconds of silence, Chip responded, "Let me get this right. You want me to stand up in front of 100-plus Millennials and tell them how managers perceive their generation?" Ron insisted that they would love it and that it would be highly beneficial for them to understand what they were about to face in the workplace. Ron was right. We are not sure how much they loved being told how they were perceived, but the knowledge was invaluable in helping them understand what they were experiencing and why. Here are a few comments from the event's feedback survey:

> "Even though the topic was about our generation, I feel like it was very eye-opening to hear the perceptions that older generations have toward us and to learn how I can work with my co-workers more effectively."

> "Very helpful and obviously related to me and my generation."

> "I liked learning how other generations view one another."

"The program shed light on the assumptions some managers have about me based on my generation. The skills are very helpful."

"It helped me to become more self-aware."

"This will change how I approach my relationships with older co-workers."

"I had never really thought about the differences between generations, and this really shed some light on it for me."

Before we list the challenges Millennials encounter, it is important to lay out an explanation for why we believe the challenges exist.

Since perceptions have the potential to create reality, we were interested in how Millennials would experience entering the workforce. Our first study was deductive, meaning we started by observing a phenomenon (generational tension in the workplace) and then developed a theory (certain competencies can reduce generational tension). The second study was inductive in that we started with a theory (perceptions of Millennials can create barriers for them at work, but those barriers can be overcome with understanding and certain skills) and worked toward a phenomenon (Millennials understanding the challenges, using the skills, and thriving as a result). Below, we list each reported challenge with its definition in descending order by frequency of response (e.g., lack of experience was mentioned more than any other challenge).

Lack of Experience

Millennials are keenly aware that they lack work experience, and they know the limitations this places on them with respect to getting what they want.

Not Being Taken Seriously

Millennials consider themselves to be problem-solvers and innovators but get frustrated when their ideas are not entertained or are readily dismissed.

Not Getting Respect

Millennials have the experience of being treated differently just because of age. They talk about not being readily accepted into the culture of the company because they are young. They are made to feel that they do not belong in important work situations.

Being Perceived as "Entitled"

Older workers think that Millennials want everything to be handed to them without their having to earn it.

Lack of Patience

Millennials have high expectations about the speed of career development and have difficulty being patient when they are not progressing as fast as they think they should.

Getting Helpful Feedback

Millennials face frustration when feedback is nonexistent, untimely, or vague.

Understanding Expectations

Millennials are confused about what is expected and experience a mismatch of expectations.

Miscommunication with Older Workers

Millennials have difficulty when it comes to communicating with older workers. They have a different communication style from other generations due to technology.

Rigid Processes

Millennials' overemphasis on processes inhibits working faster, smarter, and more effectively. They perceive existing processes to be rigid when they want to focus on the outcome.

Proving Value

Millennials want to prove their value to management. In particular, they wonder how assertive to be when it comes to asking for more responsibility or opportunity.

Understanding Corporate Culture

Millennials are uncertain about what is appropriate at work in terms of communication style, dress code, socializing, and unwritten rules. They often have trouble knowing when to be formal and when it is okay to be informal.

Challenges Created by Perception

Again, perceptions are not reality, but they can create reality when acted upon. The challenges Millennials face are very real. In Table 9.4, we draw a connection between managers' perceptions and challenges Millennials face in the workplace.

Table 9.4   Comparison of Manager Perceptions of Millennials and Challenges Millennials Face in the Workplace[4]

Manager Perceptions of Millennials	Challenges Millennials Face in the Workplace
Autonomous	Rigid processes
Entitled	Being perceived as entitled
Imaginative	Rigid processes and proving value
Self-absorbed	Not getting respect and not being taken seriously
Defensive	Getting helpful feedback
Abrasive	Miscommunication with older workers

Manager Perceptions of Millennials	Challenges Millennials Face in the Workplace
Myopic	Lack of experience and understanding corporate culture
Unfocused	Understanding expectations and priorities
Indifferent	Lack of patience

If something is considered a roadblock or barrier, it is because it is delaying or keeping the person from something he or she desires. Pay close attention to what Millennials want. Table 9.5 compares the challenges Millennials face with what they want from the workplace.

Table 9.5   Challenges Compared with What Millennials Want[5]

Challenges	What Millennials Want
Lack of experience	To have more opportunity
Not being taken seriously	To be listened to
Not getting respect	To be accepted
Being perceived as entitled	To be rewarded for work
Lack of patience	To be promoted faster
Getting helpful feedback	To know how they are doing
Understanding expectations	To know what is expected of them
Miscommunication with older workers	To have a good relationship with older workers
Rigid processes	To have a say in how they do their job
Proving value	To be recognized

Table 9.5 is a manager's playbook. Not only does it give you insight into what hinders Millennial engagement and development, but it also gives you a list of motivating factors. Think about the challenges: You have influence over most of what they find challenging. You can take them seriously. You can respect them. You can give them feedback. You can recognize them. The great thing is that there are things both you and they can do! In Table 9.6, we have listed the challenges and the strategies Millennials can use to overcome roadblocks.

Table 9.6 Comparing Challenges with Strategies for Overcoming Challenges[6]

Challenges	Strategies for Overcoming Challenges
Lack of experience	Identify people with experience (mentors) and ask them a lot of questions.
Not being taken seriously	Take responsibility for everything you control (communication, work, dress).
Not getting respect	Be respectful.
Being perceived as entitled	Show gratitude and express appreciation.
Lack of patience	Try to understand your manager's perspective and keep being persistent in your effort.
Getting helpful feedback	Ask specific questions about your performance.
Understanding expectations	Ask what is expected, listen, and then tell them what you heard them say.
Miscommunication with older workers	Build a relationship by taking an interest in them.
Rigid processes	Do it their way effectively and then offer your ideas for improvement.
Proving value	Align your strengths with the organization's needs.

Consider the strategies in Table 9.6 as discussion topics for coaching, mentoring, and development with your Millennial employees. As an example, one of the frustrating things managers face is doing something nice for an employee and having the employee not acknowledge it. The employee's lack of acknowledgment leads to the perception of entitlement.

An attorney friend of ours named Ken has a client whose company has grown significantly over the past five years. The company is led by a CEO in his early 30s. Ken is intrigued by the fact that there is not a person over 35 years old in the organization and that the CEO pays for everybody's lunch every day. One day when Ken was in the office, he noticed a basket filled with Girl Scout cookies in the break room. The

CEO had provided his daughter with prime product placement. The sign on the basket read: "Girl Scout Cookies $5. Thanks for your support!" Without hesitation, Ken reached into his pocket, pulled out a $5 bill, placed it in the envelope, and happily collected his Thin Mints. On a visit a week later, Ken noticed that the basket was still full of cookies. He thought about buying every box, but he started to think about how the CEO provided everybody's lunch, and this was the perfect opportunity for the employees to reciprocate the generosity of the CEO. It bothered Ken so much he asked the CEO if he noticed that no one was buying the cookies. The CEO did notice and replied, "I am not mad, I am hurt."

The best way to overcome the challenge of being perceived as entitled is to show gratitude and appreciation. One form of showing gratitude is reciprocation. When somebody does something nice for you, do something nice in return. We tell Ken's story frequently in new-hire onboarding events and ask for feedback from the participants about why someone would walk by the cookies everyday on their way to a free lunch and decide not to buy a box. The responses have ranged from "We don't carry cash" to "We don't have kids so we don't think about it." The coaching is easy here: Stop at the ATM on your way to work, and you don't have to have a kid to know that peoples' kids are important to them.

Showing gratitude is a great place to lead by example. If your boss does something nice for you, bring in your employees and ask them to help you decide on how you will show your appreciation.

In the next section, we suggest more coaching strategies you can use to help your Millennial employees overcome barriers they face.

Coaching Millennials to Overcome Career Roadblocks

We began the chapter with a tip about giving advice: Start with the experience of your employee. The best place to start is with what she considers to be strengths or advantages she brings to her job. If she struggles with identifying strengths, have her take Tom Rath's Strengths-Finder 2.0 inventory.[7]

Though many have espoused the merits of building on a strength over mastering a weakness, Marcus Buckingham and Don Clifton popularized the concept in their book *Now, Discover Your Strengths*.[8] The concept is rooted in psychology. People respond positively to affirmation and bristle at criticism. In botany-speak, it is called heliotropism: Plants turn into the direction of the sun. This thinking has even influenced research methodology. The method is referred to as appreciative inquiry, and the principle is the same: As a sunflower turns toward the beaming rays from the sun, people turn toward the positive. Therefore, it is a good idea to begin with what is right or good; don't ignore weaknesses but also don't allow them to dominate the agenda. Beginning with a strength builds psychological stamina.

One of the interview questions we used in our study to identify challenges Millennials face was, "As a young worker, what advantage do you think you have in the workplace?" We asked the question because when it came to designing training, we wanted to identify where we could build psychological stamina. The answers we received are rank ordered in Table 9.7, according to frequency of response.

Table 9.7 Advantages Millennials Believe They Have in the Workplace Due to Their Age[9]

Advantages
1. Technological savvy
2. Fresh education
3. Energy
4. Social networking ability
5. Flexibility
6. Global mind-set
7. Creativity

8. Teachable
9. Tolerant
10. Goal-oriented

You may find the advantages list in Table 9.7 useful for your own development and a language for demonstrating value you bring to the organization. The strengths are a great place for starting a development conversation with your employees.

One strength that is not on the list is team-oriented—perhaps because Millennials do not perceive it to be a differentiator with respect to advantage. Maybe they don't know it, but it is a differentiator, so maximize their ability to work in teams.

Managing Millennial Teams

If ever there was potential for creating hot groups, it is with Millennials. Jean Lipman-Blumen and Harold Leavitt define the *hot group* state of mind as "task obsessed and full of passion. It is always coupled with a distinctive way of behaving, a style that is intense, sharply focused, and full bore. It is contagious single-mindedness, that all-out dedication to doing something important."[10]

Focus the team's energy, passion, enthusiasm, intensity, style, and uniqueness on doing something special. Lipman-Blumen and Leavitt suggest that there are three types of hot group leaders. The first is an orchestra *conductor*; this leader is connected and hands-on day-to-day. The second is a *patron*; patrons are not hands-on or participative in team activities, but they champion the efforts of the team and keep them in good standing with the Mothership. The third is *keepers of the flame*; they build the conduit for ideas and projects to flow from one stage to another (between teams and varying projects).[11] You probably play the role of conductor at this stage of your career.

Limpan-Blumen and Leavitt give insight into how to lead a hot group:[12]

- Think and act people first, not task first.
- Part of leadership is a dramatic art, so use your whole self, your persona.
- Find ways to make an existing task more worthy.
- When possible, keep your group in an underdog position.
- Hot groups need deadlines and other routine markers.
- Develop a sense of community.
- Do your best to provide your group with generous time for breathing.
- Don't try to keep your group running full-throttle all the time.
- Keep an eye out for burnout.
- Expect periods of doubt, drought, depression, and dissension.
- Manage meaning.

Millennials want to find meaning in their work, and they want to make a difference. They want to be listened to. They want you to understand that they fuse life and work. They want to have a say about how they do their work. They want to be rewarded. They want to be recognized. They want a good relationship with their boss. They want to learn. But most of all, they want to succeed.

The keys to helping Millennials succeed:

- Value a relational approach.
- Focus on career development.
- Assure them of the relationship when things get difficult.
- Give frequent and timely feedback.
- Sponsor them for new opportunities.
- Encourage their voice.

- Help them understand the organization's culture.

- Work *with* them.

In the next chapter, we discuss managing Gen Xers, Baby Boomers, and members of the Silent generation.

Endnotes

1. Espinoza, C., Ukleja, M., & Rusch, C. (2010). *Managing the Millennials*. Hoboken, NJ: John Wiley & Sons.

2. Espinoza, C., Ukleja, M., & Rusch, C. (2010). *Managing the Millennials*. Hoboken, NJ: John Wiley & Sons.

3. Espinoza, C., Ukleja, M., & Rusch, C. (2010). *Managing the Millennials*. Hoboken, NJ: John Wiley & Sons.

4. Espinoza, C. (2012). Millennial integration: Challenges millennials face in the workplace and what they can do about them. http://rave.ohiolink.edu/etdc/view?acc_num=antioch1354553875.

5. Espinoza, C. (2012). Millennial integration: Challenges millennials face in the workplace and what they can do about them. http://rave.ohiolink.edu/etdc/view?acc_num=antioch1354553875.

6. Espinoza, C. (2012). Millennial integration: Challenges millennials face in the workplace and what they can do about them. http://rave.ohiolink.edu/etdc/view?acc_num=antioch1354553875.

7. Rath, T. (2007). *Strengthsfinder 2.0*. New York: Gallup Press.

8. Buckingham, M., & Clifton, D. O. (2001). *Now, Discover Your Strengths*. New York: Free Press.

9. Espinoza, C. (2012). Millennial integration: Challenges millennials face in the workplace and what they can do about them. http://rave.ohiolink.edu/etdc/view?acc_num=antioch1354553875.

10. Lipman-Blumen, J., & Leavitt, H. J. (1999). *Hot Groups: Seeding Them, Feeding Them, and Using Them to Ignite Your Organization*. New York: Oxford University Press.

11. Lipman-Blumen, J., & Leavitt, H. J. (1999). *Hot Groups: Seeding Them, Feeding Them, and Using Them to Ignite Your Organization*. New York: Oxford University Press.

12. Lipman-Blumen, J., & Leavitt, H. J. (1999). *Hot Groups: Seeding Them, Feeding Them, and Using Them to Ignite Your Organization*. New York: Oxford University Press.

10

Managing Boomers, Xers, and Silents

A recent Ernst & Young survey found that 72% of respondents expressed general discomfort with younger managers supervising older employees.[1] If you are a manager, then almost certainly you will be managing employees who are in their 40s, 50s, 60s, and even 70s. If you are a Millennial, then an older worker could be a Gen Xer, a Baby Boomer, or a member of the Silent generation. Each of these generations has different needs and goals.

Younger supervisors might be afraid of managing older employees who have more experience than they do. Millennial managers are likely to feel that they do not have the experience necessary to justify insisting that they know the best way to perform a given task. And as we have seen, older workers may resent being managed by someone younger, especially if that manager has less practical experience.

As Megan Johnson and Larry Johnson note in their book *Generations, Inc.*, the problem of younger supervisors managing older workers has been vexing the armed services for many decades. Because officers are generally commissioned shortly after completing a bachelor's degree, the military has had to figure out how to make the younger supervisor/older worker relationship function. Newly commissioned officers are taught to recognize and appreciate the expertise and experience of the older sergeants who report to them. Young officers are trained to treat their more experienced subordinates as partners. The hierarchical nature of the military prevents open dialog in front of lower-ranking soldiers, so sergeants are encouraged to share their experience-based opinion in private. "The supervisor is still in charge, but he's missing an opportunity (and is more likely to make a mistake) if he doesn't check in with his more experienced subordinates—at least to hear their thoughts—before making important decisions. The supervisor still sets the goals and holds people accountable for meeting them. But the subordinates have a big say in the execution, and when they walk out of their private meetings with their managers, they need to be on the same page."[2] This approach leverages the experience of the older worker, creates better outcomes for the unit, and builds a stronger, more functional relationship between the manager and the worker.

Most of the academic and practitioner literature that addresses managing older workers focuses on two areas: the issues of ageism and age-related stereotypes, and practical issues related to retaining and engaging people near or past traditional retirement age. The practitioner literature also includes a small number of books and articles devoted to the issue of Millennials managing Xers and Boomers, as well as Silents, which we summarize below.

Although the following guidelines are meant to help, keep in mind that everyone is an individual. What works for one Boomer or Gen Xer might not work for another. Because you can't count on an individual to always behave according to his or her generational profile, it is important to listen and to be open minded.

As Herb Kelleher said in a WOBI talk,[3] people work primarily for psychic satisfaction. If their work environment does not provide the psychological satisfaction they seek, workers will become disengaged. Or they might leave. This is especially true when workers are approaching retirement.

Recommendations for Managing Workers Older Than Yourself

We have a set of recommendations that should be kept in mind when managing workers older than you, regardless of their generation. These are good, general bits of advice for almost any managerial context, but they are especially poignant in a multi-generational management context, and particularly when a manager is responsible for employees who are older and more experienced than him- or herself. The next section examines specific likes, dislikes, and needs of each generation.

Know What They Don't Like

This might be even more important than knowing what motivates your Gen X, Boomer, and Silent employees. Frederick Herzberg was the first to note that things that demotivate us are usually not the opposite of the things that motivate us.[4] Herzberg referred to these demotivating factors as "hygiene" factors to help clarify that they are not on the same spectrum as motivating factors. For example, a Gen Xer might be especially sensitive to being micromanaged. If her manager is guilty of this sin, then almost certainly she will feel unhappy in her current work environment. But if one day her supervisor woke up and decided to let her get her work done on her own, she would not suddenly feel excited about her job, unless there was some other factor responsible for creating that sense of excitement that the micromanaging had been masking. If you want your employees to be engaged, then it is critical to get rid of the environmental factors that are causing them to count the minutes until they can run out the door. Also, don't make the mistake of thinking that because your firm has a lot of motivating factors, there can be no hygiene factors. This can create a confusing situation for manager and employee alike. Employees will feel torn. They may stay because of the positive factors but will complain about the negatives, demoralizing themselves and others.

Understand What Motivates Them

As we discussed in Chapters 6, "Generational Differences: Fact or Fiction?," and 7, "Dynamics of a Multigenerational Workforce," each generation has its own likes and dislikes. Keep in mind that something that motivates a Baby Boomer might not work for an Xer. We go into more detail about motivating factors for each generation later in this chapter.

Seek Their Input, Learn from Them, and Encourage Mentoring

In our survey, the number-one challenge for Millennial managers identified by both younger and older workers is lack of experience. Older workers are happy to share their experience, especially once you have shown that you value the wisdom and perspective they can offer. Sometimes a formal arrangement like a mentoring program can help to create a relationship that might not otherwise exist. When I was in fourth or fifth grade, I was given an assignment to interview an older person about his or her experience during the Great Depression. I interviewed my next-door neighbor, a man I had always liked and admired. He was a very private man whom I observed from a distance while he was busy in his garden almost every day but with whom I rarely interacted, partly because of our age difference and partly because of our communication style. He gladly accepted the request for the interview and shared with me a part of himself that I would never otherwise have gotten to experience. I wasn't much of a psychologist at that age, but the experience seemed cathartic for him, and it was deeply educational for me. I knew infinitely more about my neighbor after an hour of sharing than I had learned in the previous five years. Most mentoring arrangements will not offer the same level of intimacy, but they do create levels of education and mutual understanding that would not otherwise exist.

Communicate

Be clear about expectations and whether those expectations are being met. Provide feedback but be aware that not all groups need or want as much feedback as others. Millennials prefer to receive feedback far more frequently than Xers or Boomers. As we found in our review of the Canadian Conference Board data[5] (refer to Chapter 7), multigenerational work environments are rife with mutual misunderstanding. The only way to avoid misunderstanding is to provide an open channel for two-way communication.

Be a Leader but Don't Overdo the "Boss" Thing

Because of your position, people are looking to you to provide guidance. They expect you to make decisions and to ensure that those decisions are executed. But you do not need to be heavy-handed.

The foregoing are applicable for employees of all generations. The following sections cover issues that are specific to each generation.

Generation X

As we explained in Chapter 6, Xers were the latchkey kids, raised by Baby Boomers and Silents who were either working long hours, divorced, or pursuing their inner journey. They grew up without an authority figure present and are therefore self-reliant and prefer to be managed with a hands-off style. In this section, we list what works for Gen X employees.

Challenge them. Xers have a strong independent streak. They don't look at the office as a place to develop attachments, which means they probably won't be interested in your team-building parties. That doesn't mean they aren't interested in what they do. On the contrary, they want to be capable and competent, and they don't mind putting in the effort necessary to build up their abilities. So give them challenging assignments and then go worry about something else. Your Gen X employees will appreciate the confidence you have shown in them and the opportunity to tackle a problem on their own. Feedback is important, of course. However, you will find that most Xers are fairly blunt about their own work. Let them tell you what went well and what did not.

Help them prepare for their next job. Yes, you heard that right. It might be the best way to keep them. It may seem paradoxical, but you will actually find your Gen X workers far more engaged and a lot more loyal if you give them opportunities to develop marketable skills. Xers were the ones who saw their parents laid off, even after their parents put in long hours. Consequently, they feel it is critical to stay current in the latest techniques and technologies. They appreciate opportunities to build up their skill sets and keep their resumes current. Provide as much training as time and budget allow.

In the same vein, it is important to give them opportunities to work in different settings or different aspects of a project. For example, if you manage a software development team, you may find that some team members value the opportunity to have a break from programming to take on the role of scrum master or big data engineer. Allow them to explore new directions. You are likely to find your Xers energized and raising the collective skill level of your team.

Xers like to get things done. Processes and policies that impede progress will lead to reduced job satisfaction. Be prepared to explain why a given procedure is necessary. If it is not truly necessary, eliminate it. Better yet, give the job of revising and streamlining the official Policy & Procedure to an Xer. More will get done, and your Xer employees will feel more satisfied. They might even appreciate it.

Recognize people appropriately for their contributions. Reward and promote based on accomplishment and contribution. Xers respect leaders and coworkers who "carry the goods." Xers are particularly turned off by promotions that aren't earned and by the prominence of individuals in an organization who are not contributing. This is a huge hygiene factor for Gen X employees. For a refresher on this topic, see the classic Xer movie *Wayne's World*.

Another thing we pointed out in Chapter 6 is that Boomers were raised to be social, but Xers were not. Xers were left to their own devices as children to a much greater extent than Millennials, Boomers, or Silents. As a consequence, they are more socially awkward, as depicted by the character Garth in *Wayne's World*. But they also value authenticity. It is important for Xers to be themselves, even if that means being a little different. On the other hand, be ready to explain and even coach them on office politics.

Although Xers like getting the work done, it is not the central focus of their lives. Hence, Xers seek flexibility in their schedules. Both male and female Xers place their children's needs foremost. Xer dads want to coach their daughter's soccer team and son's baseball. Xers' parents worked long hours and missed important milestones in their lives. To Gen Xers, this just does not make sense. It also does not make sense to them that work has to be entirely serious. Xers can be intense about the quality of their work while also making it fun.

Baby Boomers

Baby Boomers have decades of work experience under their belts. However, as we saw in our review of the Canadian Conference Board survey results (refer to Chapter 7), there are several areas where Boomers' self-perceptions are at serious odds with the way Millennials see them. Boomers were raised to believe in themselves, in prosperity, and in possibilities.

A recent study by Bankers Life found that 60% of retired Baby Boomers who have a job chose to work for non-financial reasons. Eighteen percent said they chose to work in order to stay mentally sharp, 15% said they wanted to keep physically active, and 14% said they were working in order to have a sense of purpose. The same study found that among working retirees, 78% reported feeling at least as satisfied in their post-retirement jobs as they were prior to retirement, even though their post-retirement compensation was less than what they had been earning previously.[6] We are not sharing these statistics in order to suggest that all Baby Boomers are retiring imminently or that they are all seeking part-time jobs but to show the value they place on psychic satisfaction and purpose.

Baby Boomers are idealists who set out to change the world. They want their contributions at work to echo the movements they supported in their youth and later years. Many Boomers, especially members of the so-called First Wave, take social contribution seriously. They are well aware of the sacrifices that their elders made to win the war against Nazism in Europe and to fight racism and poverty at home. They heard John F. Kennedy when he said "ask not what your country can do for you but what you can do for your country." They seek to make the world more harmonious. The fact that those efforts sometimes seem misguided to non-Boomers does not in any way diminish the earnest desire to make the world a better place that motivates them. Continue to ask them to help make a difference.

Look for new ways to leverage their strengths. As we saw in Chapter 7, Boomers have an elevated view of their skills. Find ways to bring their contribution in line with their self-view. Give them positive opportunities to put their strengths to work but at the same time hold them accountable when there are gaps.

Boomers are likely to see you as being too young for your role. Don't ignore them. Unless you face their resistance squarely, they will see you as "part of the problem"—an old Boomer catchphrase. You may need to prove yourself to them through your performance. Based on what we know about you so far, this should be a snap.

Just like the Silents (described in the next section), Baby Boomers have a wealth of experience. Where possible, recruit Boomer employees to be mentors for other members of your team.

Silent Generation

Members of the Silent generation now represent around 5% of the U.S. workforce. Some authors have made a convincing claim that because of the good work habits and attitudes of workers from this age group, employers ought to seek ways to employ more of them.[7]

Herb Kelleher's observation that workers seek psychic satisfaction is especially poignant here. Traditionalist workers are more likely to be working out of a need for a sense of purpose than due to economic necessity. According to Peter Cappelli, "Older workers tend to be in the workforce because they want to be—relatively few look for jobs because they need them to survive. (During the Great Recession, we heard a lot about people not being able to retire because of finances, but we're hearing that less now.)"[8]

Cappelli adds, "Younger supervisors may find that what works with most of their staff doesn't work for older employees. They aren't as fearful of being fired (they're already at retirement age) and they have less interest in promotions or a big payout in the future."[9]

Cappelli has several recommendations for keeping Silent generation workers engaged. First, acknowledge their experience. "Everyone wants their expertise to be recognized, especially by the boss. But with older workers, it's even more important, because they typically have a lot of experience—so ignoring it is especially irritating. And older workers themselves can be prickly about being managed by someone who knows less than they do."[10]

Silent employees might not be current with the latest technology or processes, but that does not mean they don't want to be. Find out what they are capable of doing and help them adapt to and embrace new systems and methodologies.

Silents will appreciate opportunities to contribute to their departments and employers. Mostly they are looking for meaningful work. Recognize their experience and contributions by giving them opportunities to mentor younger workers.

Because of their distinct life courses, each generation has its own set of needs in the workplace. Members of all generations need to be valued—but each in a unique way. Silents and Boomers want their experience to be appreciated and to make meaningful contributions. Xers need to be challenged and to be given assignments that broaden their skill sets. Knowing what motivates and demotivates members of each generation will enable you to keep your employees engaged and productive.

In the next chapter, we list a number of challenges that managers often fall into and show you how to work your way through them so your career can really take off.

Endnotes

1. Ernst & Young, LLC. (2013). Younger managers rise in the ranks: EY study on generational shifts in the workplace. http://www.ey.com/US/en/Careers/Fall-2013-Edition-of-EY-Navigator---6---Younger-managers-rise-in-the-ranks.

2. Johnson, M., & Johnson, L. (2010). *Generations, Inc.: From Boomers to Linksters—Managing the Friction Between Generations at Work*. New York: AMACOM.

3. Kelleher, H. (2008). Building a people-focused culture. Paper presented at World of Business Ideas (previously HSM). https://www.youtube.com/watch?v=oxTFA1kh1m8.

4. Herzberg, F., et al. (1959). *The Motivation to Work* (2nd ed.). New York: John Wiley.

5. Conference Board of Canada. (2009). Winning the "Generation Wars": Making the most of generational differences and similarities in the workplace. https://www.aqesss.qc.ca/docs/pdf/i-media/20091126/ConferenceBoard_Compete_Generation_Wars.pdf.

6. Bankers Life. (2015). New expectations, new rewards: Work in retirement for middle-income Boomers. http://www.centerforasecureretirement.com/media/65648/work-in-retirement-report-may-2015.pdf.

7. Johnson, M., & Johnson, L. (2010). *Generations, Inc.: From Boomers to Linksters—Managing the Friction Between Generations at Work*. New York: AMACOM.

8. Cappelli, P. (2014). Engaging your older workers. *Harvard Business Review* blog, https://hbr.org/2014/11/engaging-your-older-workers/.

9. Cappelli, P. (2014). Engaging your older workers. *Harvard Business Review* blog, https://hbr.org/2014/11/engaging-your-older-workers/.

10. Cappelli, P. (2014). Engaging your older workers. *Harvard Business Review* blog, https://hbr.org/2014/11/engaging-your-older-workers/.

Getting to the Next Level

"Invest in yourself before you expect others to invest in you."

—Chip Espinoza

Our hunch is that you didn't pick up this book just to be a better manager at your present position. You read it because it is a part of your master plan to get to the next level. That is what we love about you. Know this: You do not need a position or title to start leading at the next level.

A Baby Boomer assistant manager from an organization we consulted asked to meet for lunch. His boss had recently resigned, and he wanted an endorsement for the position. When asked what would make him a viable candidate, he responded with a litany of things he would do. Though awkward, we had to ask, "Why aren't you doing all of this now?" He said he didn't have the title to lead—it wasn't his job. He didn't get the endorsement or the position. Ironically, a Millennial who was already going above and beyond his responsibilities received the promotion. Don't promote people for what they say they are going to do; promote them for what they are doing.

Back Where We Started

It has now been over 10 years since we began our work on understanding Millennials in the workplace, and we have stayed true to committing to a discussion with Millennials rather than a conversation about them. It has been a humbling experience to speak all over the world and address what is perceived to be one of the hottest, if not sexiest, management topics in years. In this chapter, we want to take you back to the classroom and discuss thoughts and perspectives that can be career differentiators. Although we have attempted to create a nice readable flow for the chapter, it is meant to be an imaginary Q&A with you about managerial leadership.

First, let's revisit some results from our survey. We asked employees over age 35: "What is the downside of being managed by someone under 35?" According to our survey, a perceived lack of experience is still the number-one challenge you will face as a young manager (see Table 11.1).

Table 11.1   The Downsides of Being Managed by Someone Under 35

They lack experience.
They can be immature.
They have no long-term vision.
They are too focused on their next career step.
They struggle with people skills.

Don't worry. We are not going to throw lack of experience in your face again. We bring up the survey result to point out that immaturity, lack of long-term vision, and being too focused on the next career step can be signs of impatience.

Perhaps the biggest challenge in getting to the next level now is learning patience. A lack of patience almost cost a former student her dream job. Kelly had bounced around the country, trying different jobs, until she landed at one of the world's hottest designer brand companies. After about three years of being with the organization, her boss resigned. At the suggestion of her former boss, she applied for the position. Much to her disappointment, the company brought in someone from a different region to fill the position. Kelly knew that getting the position had been kind of a long shot and accepted the decision. A year later, her new boss was reassigned back to where she had come from. Kelly applied again, only to be passed over once more. This time a person who had been at a higher level elsewhere in the company filled the position. Kelly decided that she may have hit a dead end and decided to look for a new job. She loved her company and could see herself there for a long time, but she didn't want to wait forever to be considered for the position for which she had been applying. She checked the job sites, but it took about a year before she found something worth pursuing. The week before she was going to interview for the new job, her boss asked her to lunch. It was at the lunch meeting that Kelly discovered that the two managers who were hired over her (each for one year) were brought in to help groom her for the position she desired. She had become so frustrated at what she perceived to be rejection that she failed to see the plan to advance her. She is still with the company and still moving up.

Okay, in a perfect world, Kelly knows all of this up front, and she is able to throttle her emotions and frustration back and patiently await her promotion. Companies have reasons for what they do, and actions are not always transparent. It's not a perfect world, and sometimes you have to wait. Don't sabotage yourself by being too impatient.

Managing Your Impatience

One of our Millennial managers commented, "From a cognitive perspective, I know that I am relatively young and shouldn't have such grandiose expectations of how fast I will move up, but emotionally it makes me crazy that I have to wait for waiting's sake."

Waiting is something Millennials are not accustomed to. They have grown up in a world in which they can get virtually anything from anywhere within 24 hours. More importantly, they have learned that they can advance at the pace they want. They master video games from level to level on their own clock and take Advanced Placement classes in high school to accelerate their education. They are—to some degree—*in control* of the speed of their own progress until they hit the workplace.

The ambiguity and the loss of control contribute to a lack of patience. We like to say that ambiguity is to Millennials what kryptonite is to Superman. Practicing patience when you are not completely in the "know" is an important skill if you desire to continue to advance.

So what does it mean to practice patience? In their research, Blount and Janicik suggest that patient people differ from impatient people in three key areas: the ability to evaluate why they are having to wait, understanding other people's responsibility for the delay, and taking responsibility to adapt to the situation.[1]

You may not be thrilled about it, but it is of paramount importance to make the effort to understand why you have to wait for advancement opportunities. That being said, understanding why managers are not more proactive in sponsoring advancement opportunity is difficult. As we said earlier, Millennials are accustomed to moving at their own pace. In order to practice patience, it's important for you to take responsibility for adapting to the situation in which you find yourself.

Patience requires the ability to see waiting as a necessary step toward a desired end. Here are three pieces of advice we learned in our research from the early wave of Millennials who are now finding themselves advancing at a much more tolerable pace: (1) Try to understand your manager's perspective, (2) keep being persistent in your effort, and (3) consider the waiting period as time for mastering your current responsibilities. Make the wait matter. It can be disadvantageous to your career to move at the pace that you want rather than the pace you need—which is the case when you ascend too fast.

Avoiding the "Too Much, Too Soon" Mistake

In their book *Breaking the Code of Silence*, Mitch Kusy and Louellen Essex share seven critical mistakes executives make and strategies for rebounding from them. One of the mistakes is *too much, too soon*.[2] In essence, it is accepting a position for which you are not ready. There is something very seductive and flattering about being young and being presented with opportunities normally reserved for people senior to you. Not unlike marveling at a 90-year-old who skydives, we revere a young professional who is wise beyond her years. It is a sociological phenomenon.

A former student called and wanted to have lunch. He had started with a midlevel investment firm out of college and diligently worked his way up the ladder. The CEO of the firm was stepping down and told him he was a candidate for the position. The two other candidates were 15 and 20 years older than our former student. The topic of our lunch centered on his readiness to be a CEO at age 31. The work of Kusy and Essex was helpful for the discussion. They offer the following warning signs about those who may not be ready for promotion:

- They desire success at any cost.
- They overestimate their own abilities.
- They lack emotional maturity.
- They lack self-awareness.
- They cannot self-regulate their behavior.

The fact that the student solicited and listened to feedback from a former professor and mentor was a very positive sign. He was practicing "exploring your autobiography" (refer to Chapter 5, "Be True to Others"). He easily listed his liabilities in light of the strengths of the other candidates without minimizing his own readiness. His self-critique and willingness to accept critical feedback showed his emotional maturity. Oh, by the way, he is killing it as the new CEO. He epitomizes the phrase *wise beyond his years*, but his real strength is demonstrating emotional maturity beyond his years.

Being Self-Giving Rather Than Self-Protecting

In an environment that is stressful, you will see self-protecting behaviors from all parties. Self-protecting is primarily a defensive posture aimed at protecting self-integrity. It is quite appropriate and healthy to protect the self when there is a threat. However, self-protecting can become maladaptive to the extent that it inhibits learning from important, though threatening, experiences and information. A continual effort to protect self-integrity threatens the ability to have relationships with others—particularly those with whom we may disagree.

Some signs of self-protecting behavior are refusing to listen to a perspective that is different from your own, reframing events to put yourself in a better light, projecting blame onto others, being unwilling to make apologies, and failing to take responsibility for one's own actions.

Conversely, self-giving behavior is placing attention on, and working toward, the interests of others. It involves things like being willing to listen to a different point of view, being vulnerable, and taking ownership for your actions.

If you find yourself in self-protecting mode a lot, you may be taking yourself too seriously. Here is the litmus test:

- Do you always have to be right?
- Do you argue points you are not sure of?
- Do you insist on having the last word?
- Do you find it painful to apologize?

A clear advantage that self-giving leaders have over those who self-protect is the ability to embrace resistance or people who think differently from them.

Embracing Resistance

Change is the dance between the people with the most responsibility in an organization and those who feel most vulnerable or dependent.[3] You have heard it said that leadership is influence. A particular instance of a leader applying influence is known as an *influence attempt*. Gary Yukl defines an influence attempt as the process by which a leader influences attitudes, perceptions, behaviors, or some combination of these. He shows that there are three possible qualitative outcomes of an influence attempt: commitment, compliance, and resistance.[4]

It is obvious that the desired outcome of an influence attempt is commitment. Commitment engenders devotion and dedication that is self-sustained. It's not about leaders keeping people fired up but about people keeping themselves fired up. Norman Shawchuck captures the concept: "People tend to support what they help to create." In essence, your followers are influenced by both your thinking and their own. Commitment takes time. That is why leaders need to be committed to their people before their people are committed to them or to their ideas.

Gary Yukl argues there are three possible outcomes when a leader makes an attempt to influence: commitment, compliance, and resistance.[5] We often ask clients to rank desirable outcomes of their influence attempts. The responses usually rank (1) commitment, (2) compliance, and (3) resistance. In reality, resistance is a better outcome than compliance. Unfortunately, however, it is far too common for leaders to settle for compliance. Compliance is characterized by a passivity that lends no energy to a change initiative or vision and leads to organizational paralysis. Resistance is a form of engagement. When handled properly, resistance can lead to commitment.

Celebrated organizational psychologist Edgar Schein contends that 80% of people negotiate change passively; they just go with the flow.[6] We recently had the privilege of working with a group of government employees who worked for elected officials but were not politically appointed. We asked, "How do you negotiate the change of leadership every four years?" We were intrigued by their responses:

"Never talk about what worked before."

"Don't offer your opinion about what you think."

"Smile a lot, and just keep doing what you have always done."

"I don't do anything. I know I'll be here longer than them."

"Tell the new leader you like her or him better than her or his predecessor."

While passivity may allow one to survive leadership change ad infinitum, it does not create energy or creative tension. It certainly does not lend itself to collaboration or constructive conflict. Compliance is the last thing you want as a leader unless it is more important to get your way than it is to succeed.

For the true influencer, resistance is far more desirable than compliance. A good percentage of our work involves helping leaders to not just tolerate resistance but to actually embrace it. In most cases, the mindset behind commitment is similar to the mind-set behind resistance: It reflects an attitude of wanting to do something about the position in which one finds oneself. However, unlike compliance, resistance is the precursor to breakthrough.

Breakthroughs bring a fresh perspective. Personal breakthrough is a pattern we see repeated over and over in life: Resistance leads to breakthrough, and breakthrough leads to acceptance. Think about dear friends in your life who were once adversaries.

Resistance is a natural phenomenon. As Abraham Maslow observed, the human condition does not improve through contentment; it only improves through discontent. Consequently, great leadership is not characterized by compliance or the absence of resistance but rather by the ability to embrace resistance. Resistance is necessary to clarify and refine plans and ideas. In some cases, resistance is necessary to get true commitment or breakthrough.

Ironically, the passion of conviction that makes us believable can also make us unapproachable or rigid. We become so passionate about our ideas or vision that there is no room for collaboration or disagreement. Resistance can seem like a distraction or the muse of malcontents. But it can also make you a better leader.

How do you respond to resistance?

- Do you ignore it?
- Do you marginalize the resistors?
- Do you predominately surround yourself with compliant people?

Even entire companies can embrace resistance. A large multinational company was being targeted by a nongovernmental organization (NGO) that was critical of its environmental policies. Those in the company were feeling the pain of what they considered to be exaggerated claims by the NGO. They decided to fight back the negative publicity, and they started interviewing public relations firms to represent them. One executive suggested inviting the NGO for a conversation instead of spending the money on a PR battle. The company ultimately benefitted from what turned out to be free consulting from the NGO. Embracing the resistance allowed the company to satisfy the concerns of the NGO, address its own processes, and shore up its public image.

Once you address or satisfy one level of complaints, be prepared for the next.

Contentment Breeds Discontent

If the people you manage are discontent, it does not mean you are a bad leader. It sounds paradoxical, but contentment breeds discontent. Abraham Maslow suggests that once people satisfy lower-order needs (physiological), they become discontent and begin to pursue higher-order needs (psychological). The phenomenon is what he refers to as the theory of *rising expectation*. He cautions leaders against evaluating their effectiveness based on whether people are complaining or not; rather, he recommends looking at the quality of discontent. If people don't feel safe in the building or get paid in a timely manner, that is low quality of discontent (not good). It is no secret that Millennials want to find meaning in their work and become discontented if not given the opportunity to contribute (high-quality discontent). Do not get flustered when people are not happy with something. Listen for the quality of their discontent.

We know of a person who was hired as an administrator at a private preschool. She had recently earned her master's degree in early childhood education and was excited to put her ideas to work. It was not long until some of the moms started to become discontent with her philosophy. She taught her teachers to refrain from using the word *no* with the children and instead focus on redirecting behavior. Before the end of her first year, several mothers lobbied that she be fired and called for a meeting with her boss. Her boss listened intently to their displeasure with the administrator's philosophy. He then asked if the classrooms were clean, whether the playground was safe, whether the teachers were well prepared, whether the curriculum was age appropriate, and whether the children were cared for. The mothers realized that their children were attending a great school, and the philosophy of redirection was not worth losing an effective leader over.

The point is not to get discouraged if people are complaining. We are not suggesting that high-quality discontent excuses you from listening to or resolving complaints. Rather, it should give you the emotional lift and desire to embrace criticism and work to make things even better.

Recognizing Sabotage

Since we just told you about the story of the preschool administrator experiencing a mutiny, it is fitting to talk about how leaders get sabotaged by others. Edwin Friedman argues that leaders are sabotaged in three ways: by mutiny, by seduction, and by over-functioning.[7]

Mutiny is the easiest of the three to understand. It is when a group gets together and throws you overboard. It happens in the largest corporations on Wall Street to the smallest congregations in the Bible Belt. Seduction is a far more subtle strategy. People tell you how great you are and what an incredible improvement you have been over the last manager. They are quick to point out things about you that you want to believe about yourself. Their praise comes with a caution: "Don't do anything that is going to disrupt the status quo." Over-functioning is the hardest of the three sabotage strategies to identify but probably the most common.

The goal of getting leaders to over-function is to get them so busy that they cannot possibly lead. If they are busy putting out fires or reacting to crises, then they have no time for reflection or to do what matters most for the organization. That coupled with the fact that leaders are getting shorter and shorter windows of time to actually lead compounds the effect. A *Chief Executive* magazine study revealed that the average tenure of a Fortune 500 CEO is 4.6 years.[8]

A good percentage of over-functioners get something out of doing other people's jobs for them. Avoid the temptation of feeling indispensable by saving the day.[9] When you are doing someone else's job, you are not doing your own. The sooner you learn that, the better.

The following story illustrates the benefit of not over-functioning. The course Organizational Behavior 325 was set up two ways: Students could opt to take the course as individuals or as part of a team. The professor prepared two syllabi, and students voted on which option they wanted. The catch was that in the team scenario, each person was awarded a

---

team grade and not an individual grade. There was a clause in the syllabus which stated that a student could petition for a different grade from that of the team but had to write an argument that was both read and signed by teammates. Every time the course was offered, students opted for the team approach. Teams had to design fictitious organizations that became the subject for many projects throughout the semester.

One year, an accounting major, who was destined to be the school valedictorian, signed up for the management elective. She was not excited about having to depend on others for her academic accomplishment but decided to not drop the class. By midterm, she was stressed out at the lack of participation from her other two team members. She met with the professor and said, "The only reason I took this course was because I heard you were the easiest A on campus." The professor told her not to worry because there was a clause in the syllabus that allowed for a grade change. The student argued that it was the professor's job to confront her teammates and not hers.

When it came to finals, her team had a solid C. She knew her golden rope was slipping away. The professor insisted that if she wanted more than a C, she needed to confront her teammates. She ultimately did and was granted her well-deserved A. Her teammates agreed with her assessment, signed off, and thanked her for the C, with which they were happy. Years later, the student reached out to the professor through LinkedIn. She stated that she hated him for the stress he caused in the final semester of her college days but then went on to thank him for the class. As it turns out, accounting came easily to her, but being interdependent with other people did not. She was hired by a Big Three accounting firm, and her career went vertical rather quickly. She credited her ascension to having the ability to hold other people accountable for their work and not do it for them. She learned that over-functioning is a fast path to mediocrity or failure. You may want to ask yourself:

- Do I enjoy rescuing people?

- Do I take pride in doing more than others?

- Do I love saving the day?

- Do I avoid confrontation?

- Do I feel like I am the only one who cares?

One way to quit over-functioning is to develop a leadership-centric perspective.

Leadership-Centric Rather Than Leader-Centric Thinking

Before empowerment, diversity, and team, there has to be an understanding that leadership is not a person but the collective effort of everyone at every level of your organization. Thinking leadership-centric means that you see the leader as a part of the leadership of the organization but not the whole of it. It is a perspective that is extremely important to getting the best out of the Millennials. The academic term for the concept is *distributed leadership theory*. N. Bennett et al. define *distributed leadership* as "not something 'done' by an individual 'to' others, or a set of individual actions through which people contribute to a group or organization...[it] is a group activity that works through and within relationships, rather than individual action."[10] Distributive leadership is the counterbalance to the concept of heroic leadership. We use the term *leader-centric* as a synonym for heroic leadership and the term *leadership-centric* when talking about distributive leadership.

In a leader-centric organization, most of the energy and power in the organization is accessed through the CEO, principal, or coach. In a leadership-centric organization, the leader does not have to be the smartest, most talented person in the organization. Nor does she have to have the answer for every challenge that lurks around each corner. Rather, she has to nurture an environment in which other leaders are prepared to collaborate and allowed to lead when the opportunity arises.

Organizations that are overly dependent on a heroic leader will not be prepared for the future. There is a medical term for an illness caused by a physician: *iatrogenic*. The dysfunction of many organizations is iatrogenic in that it is caused by the leader's inability to think leadership-centric.

Some signs that an organization is leader-centric:

- The organization adapts to the weakness of the leader.
- Key people mimic the behaviors of the leader.
- Decision making is highly centralized.
- Meetings get canceled when the leader is unavailable.

Moving from being leader-centric to leadership-centric is not an easy transition. It may sound counterintuitive, but the best leaders trust and follow their followers.

Following Your Followers

Ronald Heifetz asserts, "Leadership must not only meet the needs of followers but also must elevate them."[11] Following your followers is one way you can elevate a follower to leadership. The concept of following your followers is not to be confused with delegating, getting out of the way, or giving credit. It requires your attention, skills, and influence to be available for assignment.

Peter Guber, director of the movie *Gorillas in the Mist*, tells of the nightmare of shooting on location in Rwanda with 200 animals that wouldn't "act." The screenplay called for the gorillas to do what was written, and when they didn't, the only option was to fall back on a flawed formula that had failed before: using little people in gorilla suits on a sound stage. It was during an emergency meeting that a young intern asked, "What if you let the gorillas write the story? What if you sent a really good cinematographer into the jungle with a ton of film to shoot the gorillas? Then you could write a story around what the gorillas did on the film." Everyone laughed and wondered what the intern was doing in a meeting with experienced filmmakers. But ultimately they did exactly what she suggested, and the cinematographer "came back with phenomenal footage that practically wrote the story for us," Guber says. "We shot the film for $20 million, half of the original budget."[12]

Guber's example is powerful in that for the betterment of the project or company, you can follow anyone at any level of your organization. Choosing when to let your followers lead is not as difficult as it may seem. Let them lead when they have a better idea, more expertise, or greater passion or when you are stuck. A vacuum of leadership has been identified in every strata of society, and a telltale sign of a vacuum is a leader being reluctant to be a follower.

If you can't follow your followers, ask yourself:

- Am I hiring the right people?
- Am I insecure?
- Am I egocentric?
- Am I really a Millennial?

Not unlike the concept of following your followers, delegation and empowerment are also leadership-centric tools.

Being an Empowering Leader

You have already seen the data in Chapter 8, "The Reasons You Will Be a Great Leader." The numbers show that Millennials are naturals when it comes to empowerment! Though empowerment and delegation are useful tools to a leader, it is important not to confuse the two. Ken Blanchard and his co-authors offer a great definition for empowerment: "The real essence of empowerment comes from releasing the knowledge, experience, and motivational power that is already in people but is being severely underutilized."[13] The goal of empowerment is to create an environment in which an individual's belief in his or her self-efficacy is enhanced. Complex, challenging, and autonomous assignments nurture a "can do" attitude in employees. The focus of empowerment is on the development of the person and not the task.

Delegation, on the other hand, is primarily focused on the distribution of responsibility and workload—not on the development of the employee. The ability to delegate is a useful skill when used correctly, but delegating things you don't want to do or busy work can be demotivating and have an adverse impact on morale.

Empowerment requires you to accurately assess the readiness level of the employee. If done incorrectly, empowerment can result in the employee being disempowered. That is exactly what happened in the following story.

The manager of a large firm was preparing to replace the document processing equipment in the company's document processing center. Don was a student of managerial leadership and constantly looked for opportunities to improve the human side of the organization. He was a big fan of the concept of empowerment and decided to create an empowerment opportunity for his workroom director Ric. They met, and Don told him since he was the person responsible for all of the equipment and the use of it, he was putting Ric in charge of selecting the next equipment service provider. Don said he would negotiate the contract once the selection had been made. Don noticed the stream of copier salespeople marching through the building daily. Decision-making time came, and Ric did a great job of reporting on the pros and cons of each service provider before presenting his choice.

The ink on the contract wasn't even dry before there were problems with the new equipment—and the service as well. Don started to hear complaints from the firm's employees about the quality of support they were getting from Ric's department. Don met with Ric to discuss the situation. Ric confessed that the new company wasn't his first choice and that he had felt pressured into the deal. Don realized that Ric's personality allowed him to be intimidated by the sales team. Even though Ric had the knowledge and technical skills to select the service provider, in that situation he did not have the personality to tell the sales team no. Don learned the hard way that empowerment is more than just giving someone the authority to make a decision. It also requires assessing competencies to make sure you are not setting up a person for failure.

When it comes to empowering, you may want to ask yourself:[14]

- Have I determined whether the person has the ability?
- Have I given the person clear boundaries in which they are accountable for results?
- Have I given the person appropriate freedom and authority?
- Have I aligned our expectations?

The Over/Under on Communication

Communication is central to any form of leadership. There are many aspects to communication, but when it comes to getting to the next level, it is important to understand that individuals need varying amounts of information based on their personality needs.

A young consultant working in a small firm found himself the target of criticism by the owner. Graham's overall work was stellar, but the owner labeled him as a poor communicator. The owner was frustrated with Graham for not being more inclusive. Most of the owner's angst revolved around not being copied on every e-mail Graham sent.

Before moving to the small firm, Graham had worked in a large company. In that job, he had made it a practice to copy his boss on almost everything he was working on. But his boss didn't want to be bothered by the little things and asked Graham to only inform about the "big" stuff. Graham resonated with that because he had a similar personality to that of his first boss in that he didn't feel slighted if he wasn't included on every detail.

Graham made the mistake many of us do when it comes to communicating: treating others the way we want to be treated. The problem is that not everybody needs the same level of inclusion on communication, meetings, or even social events. The FIRO-B (Fundamental

Interpersonal Relations Orientation) is a personality inventory that measures, among other things, one's expressed and wanted behaviors with respect to inclusion. People with high inclusion orientation seek to involve others in virtually all they do, and they have a need for you to do the same for them.

It would be easy to label Graham's new boss as a control freak, but that would be unfair. If you look into his behavior, you find that he includes the firm (from bottom to top) in decision making, hosts numerous lunches, and copies the team on most of his e-mails. Though Graham's boss would argue that his is the best way to operate, the truth is that it is driven more by personality needs than philosophy. You can be sure Graham's first boss thought his way was the best as well. People who are high in inclusion may interpret Graham's behavior as exclusive, secretive, or even subversive.

The message here is that communication needs vary by person based on each one's need for inclusion. In the case of Graham's new boss, the adjustment is rather easy: Include him in everything until he asks you not to. Although authority structure impacts the dynamic of a relationship, it is important to understand the communication needs of the people you lead.

When it comes to the over/under of communicating:

- Don't ask yourself, "What would I want to know?"

- Don't ask yourself, "How much do I think they need to know?"

- Ask yourself, "How much do *they* need to know?"

If you are high inclusion, make sure you communicate that to the people who report to you—unless you are okay with possibly being perceived as a control freak.

Most Problems Are Not Problems at All

It is critical for a managerial leader to understand the difference between a problem and a predicament. According to Richard Farson, problems happen to you, and predicaments happen because of you. Many leaders get caught in the trap of reorganizing, rehiring, and *re-everythinging* because they fail to understand that what they perceive to be a problem is not a problem at all. Problems can be solved. If you're a farmer and a tornado destroys your silos, that's a problem. You call your insurance company, contractor, and feed supplier to solve the problem. Predicaments are different in that they come about as a result of our values and can only be coped with—not resolved—until our values change.[15]

As an example, consumer debt is not a problem but a predicament. When treated like a problem, the goal is to get the debt balance to zero. You have probably heard radio advertisements suggesting that you consolidate your debt and make one easy monthly payment, with the goal of being debt free. Unfortunately, studies show that 2 out 3 people who get out of consumer debt go right back into it. This is because consumer debt is not a problem, it's a predicament: It happens because of them. The values that drive us to spend more than we make are easily recognized: instant gratification, we deserve it, makes me feel good, keeping up with others, and helping the economy. Until our values change, we can only cope with a predicament.

A former client, a publicly traded insurance company with several divisions, was struggling with a culture of silos. The divisions were not sharing leads or cross-selling insurance products. Consequently, the company was losing potential clients to competitors. The CEO was convinced that they had grown too fast and had not established a culture of knowledge sharing. He was committed to doing whatever was needed to rehabilitate the culture, including providing training at every level across the company. Training is great, but the culture of silos didn't just happen to the company. The silos were a product of a value system. There had to be a value or values driving the organization's behavior. Further investigation revealed that the company's bonus plan was designed to pit the divisions in competition with each other for financial reward. If a division cross-sold a product, it could adversely impact everyone's bonus in the division. The CEO highly valued competition and believed it was the best motivator for high performance. However, he realized that he had two competing values in this case: competition and collaboration. He decided to change the bonus plan to one of coopetition. Sharing leads and cross-selling became a part of the bonus calculation.

Here are some signs you may have a predicament:

- There is a low level of trust in the organization.
- The company is losing key players.
- There is high staff turnover.
- Employees lack commitment.
- Subordinates won't take initiative.
- The company lacks healthy conflict.
- Succession planning is done poorly.
- A problem will not go away, no matter what you do.

Change Is Everyone's Job

Have you ever heard or read something that stays with you and just won't let go? Perhaps at first you didn't agree with it or it flew in the face of convention, but over time the concept became a window in your worldview—an "oh no" that morphed into an "ah hah." We have, and here it is: "Change looks revolutionary only in retrospect."

Change is everyone's job. Change is not solely the work of the CEO and upper management. A large corporation had been suffering from decline for a decade. The executive leadership team was exhausted, defensive, and stuck. It was suggested in a meeting that the opinions and ideas of their entire workforce be solicited to inform how the company could reinvent itself. The CFO adamantly objected: "If we ask them, they will think that we don't know what we are doing." The CEO responded, "They already think that." Such a scenario is not uncommon in today's boardrooms. The reality is that the opposite is true: A leader who solicits advice, ideas, and help is held in high regard.

One could argue that the fall of the Berlin Wall is the best characterization of revolutionary change in the late twentieth century. It marked the ending of one era and the ushering in of another. Ponder this: Did the Berlin Wall come down because East Berlin's Communist Party leader Günter Schabowski mentioned in 1989 that the border would be opened for "private trips abroad"? How much did Gorbachev's "glasnost" tour stop in Germany affect things? Or Reagan calling out to Gorbachev two years earlier with his infamous, "Mr. Gorbachev, tear down this Wall!"? What was the effect of the 120,000 nonviolent demonstrators who gathered in Leipzig, Germany, for peace prayers on October 16, 1989, chanting political slogans like "Free elections," "We are staying here," and "We are the People"? And, one certainly cannot discount the sacrifice of Chris Gueffroy on February 6, 1989. He, along with at least 100 other people, were killed at the wall. Some, like Gueffroy, gave their lives. Some gave speeches and some prayed, but they all contributed to bringing down the wall. Such is the case when significant change takes place in any organization. All levels affect change. All levels play a role in change. Too frequently, too much focus is placed on formal leadership actions, and not enough attention is given to the variety of activity taking place at other levels of the organization.

The seeds or platforms for a change initiative that may reinvent or preserve your organization are possibly already in place. Rather than stress out about producing new ideas, tap into the know-how and ideas already resident in your organization.

Don't Be Afraid of Conflict

The classical management approach to conflict was to avoid it at all cost. Though the view of conflict has advanced from "let's avoid it" to "let's introduce it," many people still find themselves sick to their stomachs when they have to deal with just the thought of it. Some studies suggest that two-thirds of a manager's job is conflict related.

What are some words you would associate with conflict? Most people think in negative terms. Conflict is neither good nor bad in and of itself. It is how we respond to conflict that determines whether it is healthy or unhealthy. If we can suspend our fear of conflict, we find that conflict can present opportunity.

Interpersonal conflict can be the most threatening type of conflict for a manager. Two challenges Millennial managers report facing are the ability to be confrontational and the ability to hold people accountable. Both situations can produce a threat, which in turn creates a reaction. It is helpful to understand how conflict progresses through stages. Norman Shawchuck illustrates the concept with what he refers to as the conflict cycle, which has five stages.[16]

Stage 1: Tension Development

Tension development involves noticing something different in a relationship but being unable to put a finger on it. It is the best time to communicate the tension, but often you don't want to over-read a situation or be dramatic, so you remain quiet.

Stage 2: Role Dilemma

When you advance to role dilemma, you sense a loss of freedom in the relationship. Something is definitely different. You may find yourself avoiding the other person and even trying to figure out who's in control.

Stage 3: Injustice Collecting

Injustice collecting is the first dangerous stage of the cycle. You begin to gather every piece of evidence to support your view that the other person is bad. The conflict moves to character assassination, triangling, and mind reading. (Triangling is trying to convince others to see things your way and recruiting them to your side.)

Stage 4: Confrontation

A triggering event produces a threat so great that there is confrontation from at least one of the parties. The confrontation can range from civility to violence.

Stage 5: Adjustments

Adjustments can be win-lose, compromise, lose-leave, win-win, or stalemate. Good adjustments resolve conflict, and poor adjustments cause the cycle to start over again at the tension development stage. The speed of advancement through the cycle increases with frequency.

The best time to deal with conflict is when you feel tension or role dilemma. Unfortunately, though, by the time you advance to role dilemma, communicating can be too threatening. Also, it is important to never assume that the other party is satisfied with the adjustments made in the relationship. It is important to get verbal and emotional buy-in to agreements. Shawchuck's model is useful for helping us understand what to anticipate when we are in conflict.

The Nature and Presence of the Leader

Earlier we mentioned Edwin Friedman's assertion that it is the nature and presence of a leader that most impacts an organization. A leader's emotional processes and behaviors act as cues for others in the organization. We don't need to tell you that the atmosphere of an office or the mood of a meeting can be gauged by the temperament of the leader. We are not saying it is good or bad; it just is, and you need to be aware that your presence has an impact beyond what you could imagine.

We worked with a newly hired CEO of a midlevel medical device manufacturing company. An investment group that had recently acquired the company had recruited him. Paul was personable and highly qualified, and he got off to a great start. He was well received by a group of employees who had worked together for 15-plus years. Six months into the position, Paul started get a little pushback from his employees with respect to workload and expectations. He called us for help. He even suggested that we interview his employees to ascertain how they were experiencing his leadership.

The interviews proved to be enlightening. His employees appreciated his knowledge and skill set. They believed he could easily exponentially grow the company. However, in each interview, comments were made about how many hours Paul put in. Some thought he was trying to lead by example, while others thought he was trying to set an expectation for everybody.

After briefing Paul on the findings, he said, "I have never asked anyone to work the hours I do." He had been getting to work around 5 a.m. and leaving around 9 p.m. When asked why he put in so many hours, he closed the door, rested his face on the palm of his hands, and took a deep breath. He told us about his struggles with his marriage and home life. He had been working unbelievable hours to avoid dealing with his personal life. He had no idea that his behavior was creating a perception that his employees interpreted as an expectation to work the same hours. Even worse, employees were experiencing family problems as a result of trying to keep up with the hours he was putting in.

It is easy to minimize one's own influence. That is not bad when it comes to keeping your ego in check. But when it comes to leading, understand that your mere presence impacts the organization.

Everybody Gets Stuck

The regression of the imagination is what happens when you get stuck.[17] It means you cannot think anything could ever be any different from your current situation. We all get stuck. We get stuck in our careers, our relationships, our faith, and our personal growth.

Friedman suggests two ways to get unstuck. The first is serendipity. Something happens that you have no control over (the loss of a parent, your parents' divorce, being fired). There are people who have experienced untold tragedy and have emerged from it with new vitality for, perspective on, and love for life.

The other way to get unstuck is to go on an adventure. You don't have to sell all you have and save the rain forest, but go for it if that works for you. You can learn a new language. You can create a bucket list. You can change careers. You can go back to school. You can take a transfer overseas. And you don't have to do it all on your own. When people see you investing in your own personal development, they are going to want to invest too!

We close the book with the following piece of advice: Don't overthink your next decision. Don't put the pressure on yourself to make the perfect decision. Your next decision is only the decision before the next decision after that.

We wish you continued success in life. The next chapter is yours to write!

Endnotes

1. Blount, S., & Janicik, G. A. (2001). When plans change: Examining how people evaluate timing changes in work organizations. *Academy of Management Review, 26*(4), 566–585.

2. Kusy, M., & Essex, L. (2005). *Breaking the Code of Silence: Prominent Leaders Reveal How They Rebound from Seven Critical Mistakes.* Dallas: Taylor Trade Pub.

3. Friedman, E. H. (1985). *Generation to Generation: Family Process in Church and Synagogue.* New York: Guilford Press.

4. Yukl, G. A. (2006). *Leadership in Organizations* (6th ed.). Upper Saddle River, NJ: Pearson/Prentice Hall.

5. Yukl, G. A. (2006). *Leadership in Organizations* (6th ed.). Upper Saddle River, NJ: Pearson/Prentice Hall.

6. Couto, D. L. (2002). The anxiety of learning. *Harvard Business Review, 80*(3), 100.

7. Friedman, E. H. (1985). *Generation to Generation: Family Process in Church and Synagogue.* New York: Guilford Press.

8. Brookmire, D. (2011). Increase your chance of survival as CEO. http://chiefexecutive.net/increase-your-chances-of-survival-as-ceo/.

9. Note: Our study suggests that Millennials are more likely to rescue (help with workload) an older worker than a younger worker.

10. Bennett, N., et al. (2003). *Distributed leadership.* Nottingham: National College of School Leadership.

11. Heifetz, R. (1994). *Leadership without Easy Answers.* Cambridge: Harvard University Press. p. 24.

12. Muoio, A. (Ed.). (1998). "My greatest lesson." *Fast Company,* June–July, 82+.

13. Blanchard, K., Carlos, J., & Randolph, A. (1999). *The Three Keys to Empowerment.* San Francisco: Berrett-Koehler, p. 4.

14. Brower, M. (1995). Empowering teams: What, why, and how. *Empowerment in Organizations, 3*(1), 13–25.

15. Farson, R. E. (1996). *Management of the Absurd: Paradoxes in Leadership.* New York: Simon & Schuster.

16. Shawchuck, N. (1983). *How to Manage Conflict in the Church.* Chicago: Spiritual Growth Resources.

17. Friedman, E. H. (1985). *Generation to Generation: Family Process in Church and Synagogue.* New York: Guilford Press.

Index

A

accountability, as element of dignity, 22

achievement, as Millennial value, 93-94

acknowledgment, as element of dignity, 22

action mind-set, 19-21

adversity, dealing with

conflict cycle, 143-145

contentment and discontent, 131-132

disagreements with your manager, 30-31

following your own path, 33-34

manager perceptions of Millennials, 93-94

organizational forces, self-differentiation and, 34-35

peer relationships, changes in, 32-33

resistance, embracing of, 129-131

sabotage, recognizing, 133-135

well-differentiated people, traits of, 28-30

advice, giving of, 89-90

ageism, defined, 7-8

analytic mind-set, 19-21

appreciative inquiry, 105

assistance, seeking of, 64-70

attention, Millennial need for, 93-94

attribution theory, 71

authenticity. *See also* differentiation

avoiding comfort zones, 41-42

believing and convincing, 45

challenges of, 38-39

exploring your autobiography, 39-41

feedback, value of, 42-43

impostor syndrome, 44-45

as a personal quality, 37

returning to your roots, 41

during transitions to new roles, 43-45

work relationships and, 37-38

authority figures

differentiation from, 28-30, 33-34

disagreements with your manager, 30-31

generational differences,
63-70

relationships with, 38

**autobiography, exploration of,
39-41**

**autonomy, manager perceptions
of Millennials, 93-94, 101**

Avolio, Bruce, 3

B

Baby Boomers
age range of, 6-7, 52

characteristics of, 54-56

life course theory and, 48-51

manager perceptions by age
survey, 81-88

strategies for Millennial
managers, 117-118

workplace perceptions, survey
bias, 71-72

workplace perceptions, survey
results, 63-70, 73-75

Banister, Christina, 72

Beat Generation, 53

**benefit of doubt, as element of
dignity, 22**

Ben Franklin generation, 79

Bennett, N., 135

Bennis, Warren, 30

bias. *See also* **stereotypes; survey
results**
challenges created by
perceptions, 101-104

surveys, bias types, 70-71

workplace perception survey,
71-72

Blanchard, Ken, 137

bosses, relationships with
authenticity and, 37

differentiation from, 29-30,
33-34

disagreement with, 30-31

generational differences,
63-70

soliciting feedback, 42-43

Buckingham, Marcus, 105

Builder generation, 53-54

C

Cappelli, Peter, 119

challenged *vs.* **effective managers, 91-92**

change management
change as everyone's job,
142-143

generational differences,
63-71, 73

managerial mind-sets, 19-21

resistance, embracing of,
129-131

Clance, Pauline, 44

Clifton, Don, 105

Clinton, Robert, 39

coaching
enlisting older workers to
mentor, 114, 118, 120

feedback, soliciting of, 42-43

manager quality and, 81-88

for overcoming roadblocks,
104-106

separation phase of
mentoring, 31
strategies for coaching Millennials, 103-104, 107-108
types of mentors, 39-41
cohort theory, 49
collaboration
collaborative mind-set, 19-21
generational differences,
63-70, 74-75
hot groups, defined, 106
manager perceptions by age
survey, 81-88
managing Millennial teams,
106-108
as Millennial strength, 106
**comfort zones, avoidance of,
41-42**
**commitment, resistance and,
129-131**
communication
challenges faced by
Millennials, 98-101, 102
communication skills, value
of, 28
expressing your own voice, 30
feedback, value of, 42-43
generational misconceptions,
75-76
manager perceptions by age
survey, 81-88
manager perceptions of Millennials, 93-94, 101-104
over/under communication,
139-140

skills for managing
Millennials, 95-98
skills for managing older
workers, 115
**compliance, leadership and,
129-131**
**Conference Board of Canada,
workplace survey**
bias in, 71-72
results, 63-70, 73-75
confidence, 17
conflict, dealing with
conflict cycle, 143-145
contentment and discontent,
131-132
disagreements with your
manager, 30-31
following your own path,
33-34
manager perceptions of
Millennials, 93-94
organizational forces, self-
differentiation and, 34-35
peer relationships, changes in,
32-33
resistance, embracing of,
129-131
sabotage, recognizing,
133-135
well-differentiated people,
traits of, 28-30
**contentment and discontent,
131-132**
context, management of, 19-21

corporate culture
  culture shock of work, 90-91
  manager mind-sets, 19-21
  organizational forces, self-
    differentiation and, 34-35
  understanding of, 101
Coupland, Doug, 52, 57
culture, characteristics of,
  50-51. *See also* corporate
  culture; sociological context,
  generational differences

D

decision-making skills
  desire to please boss and, 30
  getting unstuck, 146-147
Decker, Bert, 45
delegation, 138
Deloitte, Millennial Survey, 87
demographics, generational age
  cohorts, 6-7, 52
differentiation. *See also*
  authenticity
  characteristics of, 28-29
  following your own path,
    33-34
  organizational challenges to,
    34-35
  peer relationships, changes in,
    32-33
discontent and contentment,
  131-132
distributed leadership theory,
  135-136
diversity, generational attitudes,
  64-70

E

effective *vs.* challenged
  managers, 91-92
emotional skills, 28-30
empowerment of employees,
  81-88, 137-139
entitlement, perception of,
  100-104
Espinoza, Chip, 1, 123
Essex, Louellen, 127
Expectation Hangover, 11
expectation mismatch, 100, 102
experience, level of
  managing impatience,
    125-126
  of Millennial managers, 14-15
  patience, importance of,
    124-126
  perceived value of, 89-90
  Silent generation, 119-120
  "too much, too soon" mistake,
    126-127
  workplace challenges, 99-102

F

fairness, dignity and, 22
Farson, Richard, 141
feedback. *See also* coaching
  competencies for managing
    Millennials, 96-97, 101
  value of, 42-43
  well-differentiated people
    and, 29
  workplace challenges, 100, 102

Filipczak, Bob, 52

FIRO-B (Fundamental Interpersonal Relations Orientation), 139-140

followers, value of, 136-137

formal *vs.* informal, generational differences, 64-70, 73, 93-94

Friedman, Edwin, 28-29, 35, 133, 145, 147

friendship mentors, 40

G

generalizations, 6-8

generational differences

challenges Millennials face in workplace, 98-101

demographical definitions, 6-7, 52

generational subcultures, 50-51

intergenerational communication, 75-76

life course perspective, 48-51

manager perceptions by age survey, 81-88

managing older workers, overview, 111-115

maturational perspective, 47-48

workplace perceptions, survey biases, 71-72

workplace perceptions, survey results, 63-70, 73-75

generational theory, 49

Gen Xers

age range of, 6-7, 52

characteristics of, 56-57

life course theory and, 48-51

manager perceptions by age survey, 81-88

strategies for Millennial managers, 115-117

workplace perceptions, survey bias, 71-72

workplace perceptions, survey results, 63-70, 73-75

Goffee, Rob, 27, 38-39

Google's eight managerial behaviors, 83-82

Gosling, Jonathan, 19-20

gratitude, showing of, 103-104

Great Recession (2008), responses to, 49

Guber, Peter, 136-137

H

Hanft, Adam, 79

Hassler, Christine, 11

Heifetz, Ronald, 35, 136

heroic leadership, 135

Herzberg, Frederick, 113

Hesselbein, Frances, 4

Hicks, Donna, 21-23

hot groups, 106-107

Howe, Neil, 52

hubris, 17

hygiene factors, 113

I

Ibarra, Herminia, 38, 42-44

identity, personal. *See also*
  authenticity
    dignity and, 22
    following your own path,
      33-34
    organizational challenges to,
      34-35
    peer relationships, changes in,
      32-33
    well-differentiated people,
      traits of, 28-30

Imes, Suzanne, 44

immaturity, defined, 8

impostor syndrome, 44-45

impression management, 39

inclusion, dignity and, 22

independence
  dignity and, 22
  generational differences,
    63-70
  well-differentiated people,
    traits of, 28-30

influence attempt, 129

informal *vs.* formal, generational differences, 64-70, 73, 93-94

information sharing,
  generational differences, 63-70

intrinsic values of Millennials,
  93-94

J-K

Jones, Gareth, 27, 38-39

Kahane, Adam, 42

Kelleher, Herb, 86-87, 112

Kusy, Mitch, 127

L

leader-centric mindset, 135-136

leadership
  believing and convincing, 45
  definition of, 5-6
  Edwin Friedman on, 35
  effective *vs.* challenged
    managers, 91-92
  empowering leaders, 137-139
  following your followers,
    136-137
  getting unstuck, 146-147
  hot teams, roles in, 106-107
  influence attempts, 129
  leaders, definition of, 5
  leadership-centric mindset,
    135-136
  managing Millennials, 95-98,
    106-108
  mind-sets, dignity as, 21-24
  mind-sets of managers, 19-21
  nature and presence of
    leaders, 145-146
  Ronald Heifetz on, 35
  self-differentiation and, 35
  self-giving *vs.* self-protecting,
    128

task- and relationship-
oriented leadership, 6
Warren Bennis on, 30
learning, defined, 5
learning new skills, generational differences, 64-70
Leavitt, Harold, 106-107
Lencioni, Patrick, 41
Leonard, William (Bill), 39
Le Roux, Pieter, 42
life course perspective, 48-51
life stream, 3
Lipman-Blumen, Jean, 106-107
listening skills
generational differences, 63-70, 75-76
manager perceptions by age survey, 80
loyalty to organization
generational differences, 63-70
manager perceptions of Millennials, 93-94

M
management, as whitewater rafting, 5
management, definition of, 5-6
management, transition to
advice for managers, 16-17
authenticity, maintaining, 43-45
overview of, 11
peer relationships, changes in, 12, 32-33

survey, being managed by a Millennial, 12-15
survey, Millennial managers in transition, 12
managers
definition of, 5
desire to please bosses, 28-30
dignity as a mind-set, 21-24
disagreements with, 30-31
effective *vs.* challenged managers, 91-92
employee survey results, 80-88
Google's eight managerial behaviors, 83-82
managing Baby Boomers, 117-118
managing Gen Xers, 115-117
managing Millennials, 27, 95-98, 106-108
managing older workers, overview, 111-115
managing the Silent Generation, 119-120
mind-sets of, 19-21
over-functioning, 133-135
peer relationships, changes in, 12, 32-33
perceptions of Millennials, challenges of, 101-104
perceptions of Millennials, survey data, 93-94
task- and relationship-
oriented leadership, 6
Maslow, Abraham, 131-132
maturational perspective (theory), 47-48

McGregor, Douglas, 21

meaning, as Millennial value, 93-94, 98

mentors
coaching on overcoming roadblocks, 104-106
enlisting older workers to mentor, 114, 118, 120
feedback, soliciting of, 42-43
manager quality and coaching skills, 81-88
separation phase, 31
strategies for coaching Millennials, 103-104, 107-108
types of mentors, 39-41

Meriace, Johns, 72

Millennials
age range of, 6-7, 52
challenges created by perceptions, 98-104
characteristics of, 57-59
intrinsic values of, 93-94
life course theory and, 48-51
manager perception of Millennials, 93-94
manager perceptions by age survey, 81-88
managing Millennials, 95-98, 106-108
workplace perceptions, survey bias, 71-72
workplace perceptions, survey results, 63-70, 73-75

Millennial Survey, Deloitte, 87

mind-sets of managers, 19-21

Mintzberg, Henry, 19-20

motivation, generational differences, 74

Multidimensional Work Ethic Profile (MWEP), 72

multitasking
competencies for managing Millennials, 97
definitions of, 72
generational differences in, 63-70, 72-73
manager perceptions of Millennials, 93-94

mutiny, 133. *See also* conflict, dealing with

O

organizational culture. *See* corporate culture

organizational loyalty
generational differences, 63-70
manager perceptions of Millennials, 93-94

overconfidence bias, 71

over-functioning, 133-135

P

patience
importance of, 124-125
managing impatience, 100-102, 125-126
"too much, too soon" mistake, 126-127

peer relationships
  changes in, 12, 32-33
  disagreements and, 31
  importance of maintaining, 37
People Analytics, managerial
  behaviors list, 83-82
personal identity. *See also*
  authenticity
  dignity and, 22
  following your own path,
    33-34
  organizational challenges to,
    34-35
  peer relationships, changes in,
    32-33
  well-differentiated people,
    traits of, 28-30
personality inventories,
  FIRO-B, 139-140
perspective, leadership and
  dignity as a mind-set, 21-24
  impact on people, 24
  mind-sets of managers, 19-21
Pfeffer, Jeffrey, 85
playfulness, value of, 45
power-oriented management,
  81-88
pride, 17
problems, identification of,
  141-142
procedures and processes,
  following of, 64-70, 101-102

R

Raines, Claire, 52
Ramey, Garey, 58
Ramey, Valerie A., 58
Rath, Tom, 105
recognition, dignity and, 22
redefinition stage, mentoring
  and, 31
reflective mind-set, 19-21
relationships
  competencies for managing
    Millennials, 96
  disagreements and, 31
  management of, 19-21
  peer relationships, 12,
    32-33, 37
  relationship-building skills, 28
  relationship-oriented
    leadership, 6
resistance, embracing of,
  129-131
respect, dignity and, 21-24
results orientation, 64-70, 81-88
rewards
  competencies for managing
    Millennials, 95-98
  as Millennial value, 93-94
Rhinesmith, Stephen, 19

S

sabotage, recognizing, 133-135
Sacks, Dan, 58
safety, dignity and, 22
Sanders, Tim, 89

sandpaper mentors, 40

Schein, Edgar, 130

Schultz, Howard, 24

seduction, 133

self-awareness, maturity and, 8

self-differentiation. *See* differentiation

self-efficacy, defined, 17

self-esteem, defined, 17

self-expression, as Millennial value, 93-94

self-giving *vs.* self-protecting, 128

self-management, 8, 19, 28-30

self-serving bias, 71

separation phase, mentoring and, 31

Shawchuck, Norman, 129, 144-145

Silent generation
    characteristics of, 53-54
    strategies for Millennial managers, 119-120

simplicity, as Millennial value, 93-94, 97

sociological context, generational differences, 49-51
    Baby Boomers, 54-56
    Generation Xers, 56-57
    Millennials, 57-59
    Silent generation, 53-54

Southwest Airlines, 85-86

Spock, Benjamin, 55

stereotypes, 6-8. *See also* bias; generational differences
    impostor syndrome and, 44
    workplace perceptions, overview, 63-70

Stevenson, Betsey, 58

Strauss, William, 52

strengths, identifying and building on, 105-106

StrengthsFinder inventory, 105

subcultures, generational, 50-51

supervision, need for, 64-70

survey results
    advantages of Millennials, 104-106
    advice for Millennial managers, 16-17
    being managed by a Millennial, 12-15
    generational differences in the workplace, 64-70
    manager perceptions by age survey, 81-88
    manager perceptions of Millennials, 93-94
    Millennials experience with management transition, 12
    Millennial Survey, Deloitte, 87
    People Analytics, manager behaviors, 83-81

T

task-oriented leadership, 6

teamwork

 collaborative mind-set, 19-21

 generational differences, 63-70, 74-75

 hot groups, defined, 106

 manager perceptions by age survey, 81-88

 managing Millennial teams, 106-108

 as Millennial strength, 106

technology, generational differences, 63-70

theory of rising expectation, 131-132

Theory X managers, 21

Theory Y managers, 21

"too much, too soon" mistake, 126-127

Traditionalist generation, 53-54

trust, 41

Tulgan, Bruce, 48

U-V

understanding, as element of dignity, 22

upward mentors, 39-40

Vaill, Peter, 5

value, proving of, 101-104

values of Millennials, 93-94

Veteran generation, 53-54

vulnerability, value of, 41-42

W-X

Warhol, Andy, 53

whitewater rapids, management as, 5

Wiseman, Liz, 5, 15

Woehr, David, 72

work, culture shock of, 90-91

workers

 advice for managers, 16-17

 empowerment of employees, 81-88, 137-139

 teamwork, generational differences and, 63-70

 views on being managed by a Millennial, 12-15

work-life balance, 63-70, 93-94

workplace

 challenges created by perceptions, 101-104

 challenges faced by Millennials, 98-101

 perceptions survey, 63-70, 73-75

 perceptions survey, bias in, 71-72

worldly mind-set, 19-21

Worrell, Margie, 37

Y-Z

Yukl, Gary, 129

Zemke, Ron, 52